P9-DWM-953

YOU'LL NEVER TIRE OF THE STAR OF A
HEALTHFUL DIET—SERVE **BROCCOLI** AND ITS
CRUCIFEROUS COUSINS DAILY
WITH ZEST, FLAVOR, AND EXCITING VARIETY

Hearty Broccoli Vegetable Soup

Broccoli, tomatoes, pasta, and more make this an old-fashioned, full-bodied soup. Add a slice of multigrain bread and you have a fabulous one-dish meal.

Broccoli Barley Salad Provençale

Flavored with thyme, olives, garlic, and radishes, this hearty broccoli and barley salad brings the South of France to your table—a special treat that takes just minutes to create.

Angel Hair Primavera with Creamy Tomato Sauce

This rich-tasting Italian favorite uses both cauliflower and broccoli for twice the goodness—but has surprisingly few calories and is very low in fat.

Penne with Scallops, Shrimp, and Broccoli

Perfect to serve for company or just to pamper yourself, this savory seafood dinner takes just ten minutes to prepare and cooks in just twenty. . . . Magnifico!

Chinese-style Sesame Noodles with Broccoli

A lighter version of the Chinese restaurant classic, this superquick main course blends eight great flavors into one palate-pleasing dish that children are crazy about.

LOTS OF RECIPES FOR CABBAGE, CAULIFLOWER,
BRUSSELS SPROUTS, BOK CHOY, AND KALE, TOO!

BROCCOLI POWER

TAMARA HOLT

INTRODUCTION BY
MARILYNN LARKIN

A LYNN SONBERG BOOK

Published by
Dell Publishing
a division of
Bantam Doubleday Dell Publishing Group, Inc.
666 Fifth Avenue
New York, New York 10103

If you purchased this book without a cover you should be aware that this book is stolen property. It was reported as "unsold and destroyed" to the publisher and neither the author nor the publisher has received any payment for this "stripped book."

Nutritional science and research findings about cancer prevention are constantly evolving and subject to interpretation. Although every effort has been made to include the most up-to-date information in this book, there can be no guarantee that this information won't change with time and further research. Before making any major change in their diet, readers should consult their physicians. Readers should also bear in mind that this book is not intended for the purpose of self-diagnosis or self-treatment and should consult medical professionals regarding any and all medical problems.

Copyright © 1993 by Lynn Sonberg Book Services

All rights reserved. No part of this book may be reproduced or transmitted in any form or by any means, electronic or mechanical, including photocopying, recording, or by any information storage and retrieval system, without the written permission of the Publisher, except where permitted by law.

The trademark Dell® is registered in the U.S. Patent and Trademark Office.

ISBN: 0-440-21537-4

Printed in the United States of America

This book is for all of the broccoli lovers and haters (that includes you, George Bush!). But mostly, it is for the broccoli tasters—my friends, family, and teachers who dreamed about broccoli on my behalf. Thanks to all for your ideas and encouragement. And a special thank you to Shirley King and Marie Simmons, for everything.

—*Tamara Holt*

Contents

MAIN COURSES

PASTAS, PIZZAS, AND BREADS

SIDE DISHES

WHAT YOU NEED TO KNOW ABOUT BROCCOLI POWER

Hard to believe, but true: eating vegetables may actually save your life! Recent scientific research is confirming what some scientists have long suspected; namely, that nutrients and other substances contained in broccoli (and other vegetables in the cabbage family) apparently play a key role in lowering our risk of developing cancer and other diseases.

Over the past decade, numerous studies have correlated a high intake of foods rich in vitamins A, C, and E—known as "antioxidants"—with a reduced risk of certain types of cancers, including cancers of the lung, colon, male and female reproductive systems, and the gastrointestinal tract.

Today, as scientists delve more deeply into the basic chemistry of vegetables, they are discovering other specific chemicals that act to protect human cells from cancer-causing substances.

With respect to broccoli and certain other vegetables, the latest news is very encouraging. Researchers at Johns Hopkins Medical Institutions have isolated a potent chemical called *sulforaphane* which, they predict, will prove to be among the substances responsible for blocking tumor formation in animals and people. This powerful protective substance, known as a "chemo-protector," is present in broccoli and a number of other "cruciferous" vegetables included in the recipes in this book, such as cauliflower, green cabbage, chinese cabbage (bok choy), kale, radishes, and turnips.

Now, with this book, incorporating these vegetables into your daily diet has never been simpler—or more delicious! Our recipes also follow the recommended healthy eating guidelines of the American Cancer Society, the National Cancer Institute, and other major health organizations: they're low in fat, low to moderate in calories, and high in fiber.

Of course, no single food or group of foods on its own can ward off disease. Nor obviously will eating broccoli or any other particular food guarantee you will not develop cancer or other illnesses. But the growing body of evidence in support of the health-promoting benefits of vegetables simply can't be ignored. So if you're concerned about good health, you'll want to include generous servings of a variety of vegetables in an overall healthy diet— and this book presents many creative ways to do just that. As you read through these pages, you'll learn how to turn even the most mundane veggies into tantalizing, mouthwatering delights!

WHY BROCCOLI POWER?

Broccoli was selected as the star of our cookbook because of its ever-growing popularity. Annual broccoli consumption in the United States soared 800 percent in the last two decades, from half a pound per person in 1970 to

4¹/₂ pounds per person in 1989. Today, one-third of all American households are eating broccoli at least once every two weeks, according to one study. With this book, you can turn broccoli into a main ingredient in as many meals as you wish—and the menu never gets boring. In fact, for those days when you absolutely can't eat another serving of broccoli in any form, we've included delicious recipes built around other cruciferous and sulforaphane-containing vegetables, such as cabbage, bok choy, kale, turnips, and brussels sprouts.

WHAT IF I DON'T LIKE VEGETABLES?

Many people mistakenly believe they don't like vegetables, and date their dislike to early childhood. But if you think about it objectively, vegetables often got a raw deal during our growing-up years. Although we knew back then that they were healthful, nobody told us they could also taste good. Vegetables were all too frequently prepared in ways that made them particularly unappetizing to eat: boiled and overcooked, spilled out of a can onto your plate. The fine—yet amazingly simple—art of vegetable cuisine was largely unknown.

Yet the roots of the word *vegetable* are the Latin words *vegetare,* meaning "to grow," and *vegere,* which means "to rouse, excite." Clearly, vegetables were never meant to be dull, lifeless things sitting on the sidelines of an otherwise splendid meal; rather, they are colorful, lively, snappy members of the menu, whether prepared as the main attraction or as an enhancement to a main course.

With this book, you'll learn to prepare such eye-catching palate pleasers as Red Cabbage Salad with Ginger Dressing (p. 41), Breaded Broccoli Florets with honey mustard sauce or creamy horseradish (p. 143), Broccoli with Beef and Orange Sauce (p. 63), Brussels Sprouts and Cauliflower with Curried Yogurt (p. 49), Broccoli or Kale Cheese Quiche (p. 87) and Broccoli-Ricotta Stuffed Pizza (p. 121). Incredibly, most of our recipes take only a few minutes to prepare and less than 15 minutes to cook.

Think you don't like vegetables? Try these tasty dishes and think again!

WHY YOU NEED THIS BOOK

Need more reasons to make vegetables a part of your life? We'll do our best to convince you. Although the news is out about the health benefits of vegetables (we'll explore them more completely in the next section), the sad fact is, Americans are still not getting enough of these good-for-you foods. True, broccoli consumption has increased by leaps and bounds. But that's only part of the picture. The USDA, the Department of Health and Human Services, and the National Academy of Sciences suggest that for good health we should include 3 to 5 servings of vegetables in our daily diet. Yet data from the most recent National Health and Nutrition Examination Survey (NHANES II) reveal that only 27 percent of the population consume three or more servings of vegetables daily —and a startling 23 percent eat few or no vegetables.

That's where *Broccoli Power* comes in. Our goal is to help you include this versatile vegetable—and others—in your daily menus as temptingly and easily as possible. Because once you start eating adequate servings of these and other nutritious foods, you'll quickly begin to benefit from their health-promoting powers.

In the following pages, you'll learn how the nutrients

in broccoli and other vegetables can help boost overall health and reduce the risk of cancer and other illnesses. You'll also learn how to select, store, and prepare vegetables so you get the maximum nutrient value for your money. Then you'll get to savor some of the most delicious and healthful recipes ever—prepared, tested, and tasted to perfection!

The first section is filled with recipes for savory soups —some delicate, some hearty—all rich-tasting yet low in fat. In section two, you'll learn to create wonderfully refreshing salads with brightly flavored dressings. Section three presents vegetables as an integral part of the main course—lightly stir-fried with combinations of chicken, beef, or pork; roasted with fish in a savory casserole; stewed to perfection; baked in a pie . . . there's no end to the variety of ways that crucifers can be served!

Italian food aficionados will adore section four, which features broccoli and other vegetables in pastas, pizzas, and breads. And, for those meals in which vegetables will play second fiddle, section five provides an array of tasty side dishes.

Now let's take a closer look at the health-promoting powers of cruciferous vegetables.

MEET THE MIGHTY CRUCIFERS!

Broccoli, brussels sprouts, cabbage, cauliflower, kale, radishes, and other crucifers are truly like crusaders in the battle against disease. The nutrients they contain are among the most powerful dietary promoters of good health. Once you've consumed them, they embark on their protective work.

Combatting Cancer

As we've seen, the crucifers are rich in several nutrients that may reduce your risk of developing cancer. One is sulforaphane, which may ultimately prove to be the chemical responsible for blocking tumor formation. Another is beta carotene, a form of vitamin A. Laboratory studies conducted in the United States suggest that this form of vitamin A reduces the incidence of some cancers in animals; studies conducted in Europe and Japan on people who smoke and those who have given up the habit indicate that vitamin A may reduce the risk of developing lung cancer.

Vitamin C is another potent cancer-fighter. Studies suggest that people who get plenty of vitamin C from vegetables and fruit have a lower risk of developing cancer of the stomach and esophagus.

The crucifers also have a high fiber content, and some studies have shown that colon cancer is lower in populations that consume mostly unrefined, high-fiber foods. *Why* this is the case isn't clear, however. Some scientists believe fiber itself plays a protective role. Others believe that including high-fiber foods in your diet is important because you're then less likely to consume high-*fat* foods —and a diet high in fat has been linked to the development of cancers of the breast, colon, and prostate.

There's more. Consumption of cruciferous vegetables has also been linked to a reduced risk of cancer of the gastrointestinal and respiratory tracts. Again, the exact mechanism isn't yet known. It could be that the combination of cancer combatants—sulforaphane, vitamin A, vitamin C, and fiber—is responsible for the crucifers' anticancer powers. Or, other substances in these foods—as yet undiscovered—may provide the key. Regardless of *why* they work, it's clear that incorporating ample servings of crucifers in your diet is likely to provide protection against diet-related cancers, and perhaps other cancers, as well.

You should also follow some additional dietary guidelines which may reduce cancer risk. The American Cancer Society (ACS) recommends that you avoid obesity, which is associated with increased mortality from cancers of the stomach, colon, breast, and other sites. And including fresh vegetables in your diet can help you lose pounds and maintain a desirable weight.

The ACS also recommends reducing fat intake to no more than 30 percent of your total daily calories. Excessive fat intake appears to increase the risk of developing cancers of the breast, colon, and prostate. Since vegetables contain only trace amounts of fat, you can eat as many as you like.

A variety of vegetables and fruits should be included in your daily diet, according to the ACS. And you should eat more of them because, as we've seen, many of these foods contain substances that are now being studied for their cancer-preventive properties. This book provides you with a seemingly endless variety of ways to prepare and serve vegetables.

Other guidelines from the ACS include eating more whole grain products, as well as fruit and vegetables, because of their high fiber content; limiting consumption of alcoholic beverages, since alcohol is associated with a higher risk of developing cancers of the mouth, larynx, and esophagus; and limiting consumption of smoked, salt-cured, and nitrite-cured foods, which may increase the risk of stomach and esophageal cancers.

Combatting Heart Disease

Cruciferous vegetables also play a role in fending off heart disease. For one thing, a diet rich in vegetables is less likely to be rich in artery-clogging fat. Also, there's evidence that people on high-fiber diets excrete more bile acids, sterols (including cholesterol) and fat than people on low-fat diets. In addition, fiber moves food substances through the gastrointestinal (GI) tract relatively quickly, so there's less time for cholesterol to be absorbed. Finally, recent research suggests that the antioxidant vitamins A and C, of which broccoli is an excellent source, may play a role in reducing risk of heart disease.

Many of the recipes in this book have been adapted to give you heart-healthy versions of otherwise high-fat fare. For example, the "Cream" of Broccoli Soup (p. 25) is made with evaporated skim milk; Different Cole Slaw (p. 43) is made with low-fat yogurt, instead of mayonnaise; the cheeses in the Baked Potato with Broccoli and Cheese recipe (p. 91) include cottage cheese, part-skim or nonfat ricotta and reduced-fat cheddar.

Combatting Digestive Disorders

Roughage—the old-fashioned word for fiber—really does do wonders for the digestive system. Fiber makes the intestinal muscles work to push it through, thus exercising those muscles and keeping them in good working tone. Because it absorbs water and hastens the transit time of waste through the colon, fiber helps prevent constipation. The absorption of excess water also helps prevent diarrhea. Finally, fiber promotes regularity by helping the GI muscles work properly and by keeping the GI tract mildly distended, which prevents the spasms associated with irritable bowel syndrome and other digestive disorders.

Combatting Overweight

When you begin to include the recommended 3 to 5 servings of vegetables in your daily meals, chances are you will shed at least a few pounds—more, if you've been used to eating lots of high-fat foods. The reason: the high fiber content of vegetables makes them incredibly filling. It's hard to make room for rich desserts after pigging out on vegetables.

A FEW WORDS ABOUT SUPPLEMENTS

Although we've been talking about the health benefits of specific nutrients in broccoli and other crucifers, it's important to note that these nutrients—vitamin A, vitamin C, fiber, and others—work in concert with each other within each food. For this reason, it's best to get your nutrients from food.

However, some physicians suggest taking a vitamin and mineral supplement containing no more than 100 percent of the Recommended Dietary Allowances (RDAs) of each nutrient to be on the safe side, in case your diet falls short of the daily recommendation. There is also early evidence to show that even higher intakes of some nutrients, such as vitamins A, C, and E, may provide additional cancer-fighting benefits. Always check with your physician before taking any supplements.

A POWER-PACKED PICTURE:
BROCCOLI'S NUTRIENT PROFILE

Broccoli's nutrient profile presents a pretty picture from the point of view of good health. A one-cup serving, cooked, of fresh chopped broccoli contains the following nutrients (where appropriate, the percentage of the Recommended Dietary Allowance for women and men between the ages of 25 and 50 are included):

NUTRIENT	RDA (%)	
	Female	Male
Calories: 45	—	—
Fat: .5 grams	—	—
Cholesterol: 0	—	—
Fiber: 1.7 grams	—	—
Protein: 5 grams	9	7
Carbohydrate: 8 grams	—	—
Vitamin A: 216 RE (2160 iu)	27	21
Vitamin C: 116 milligrams	194	194
Thiamin: .09 milligrams	8	6
Riboflavin: .18 milligrams	13	10
Niacin: .90 milligrams	6	5
Vitamin B$_6$: .22 milligrams	14	11
Folate: 78 micrograms	43	39
Vitamin B$_{12}$: 0 (only in animal foods)	—	—
Calcium: 72 milligrams	9	9
Iron: 1.3 milligrams	9	13
Potassium: 456 milligrams	—	—
Phosphorus: 92 milligrams	12	12
Zinc: .60 milligrams	5	4
Magnesium: 38 milligrams	14	11
Selenium: .3 milligrams	.5	.4
Sodium: 40 milligrams	—	—

[Source: USDA Human Nutrition Information Service]

As you can see, broccoli is an *excellent* source of vitamin A, vitamin C, and folate, a *good* source of fiber, protein, thiamin, riboflavin, vitamin B_6, calcium, iron, phosphorus, and magnesium, and a *fair* source of niacin and zinc.

WHY THESE NUTRIENTS ARE IMPORTANT

To better understand why broccoli's nutrient profile is so attractive, it helps to know something about the role of specific nutrients in health. Let's look at them one by one.

Calories

Calories are a measure of the energy contained in a particular food. Most of us don't have to worry about falling short on calories, so the fact that broccoli contains so few is a definite plus.

Fat

Fat is used as fuel by the body, but only as a last resort. Calories from fat tend to stay around—a holdover from humankind's prehistoric days, when fat was stored as a hedge against lean times. Today, the body's preference for retaining fat is a nuisance and a health hazard; fat has been shown to be a risk factor for breast, colon, prostate, and other cancers.

Cruciferous vegetables (which contain next to no fat) help reduce the amount of fat in our diet in two ways: the fiber they contain helps speed fat through the GI tract and out of the body, and they fill us up so we're less hungry for high-fat fare.

Cholesterol

Cholesterol is needed for the production of hormones and other substances in the body. Usually, the body produces on its own all the cholesterol necessary for health; most of us have no need to get additional cholesterol from food. Nevertheless, many of us do consume cholesterol in whopping amounts from fatty animal foods—a risk factor for heart disease.

Like all plant foods, the crucifers contain no cholesterol—provided you don't drown them in butter or rich sauces. Crucifers may also help reduce your level of blood cholesterol. The recipes in this book provide low or no cholesterol versions of the traditional cholesterol-laden accompaniments.

Fiber

We've already seen that fiber benefits the body by keeping the digestive system running smoothly and helping fend off cancer and heart diseases. The National Cancer Institute recommends that Americans double their daily fiber intake to at least 20 to 30 grams daily. Including several servings of cruciferous vegetables in your diet will help meet this recommendation.

Protein

Protein is vital for healthy cells. Yet many physicians are concerned that people are getting most of their protein from animal foods—which also contain lots of fat and cholesterol. It's important to recognize that several generous daily servings of plant foods such as vegetables can help you meet a substantial portion of your protein requirement—without increasing your intake of fat or cholesterol.

Carbohydrate

Carbohydrate is the body's main fuel. And, coincidentally, most of broccoli's calories—and those of the other crucifers—come from carbohydrate. Consequently, the small number of calories these veggies contain get used up almost immediately by the body.

Vitamin A

As we've seen, vitamin A and its various components appear to reduce the risk of developing certain cancers. This vitamin also plays a role in strengthening the immune system and staving off lesser ills. Broccoli and the other cruciferous vegetables are generally good sources of vitamin A.

Vitamin C

Like vitamin A, vitamin C is thought to reduce cancer risks and strengthen the immune system. Again, broccoli and the other crucifers are excellent sources of this important vitamin.

B Vitamins

Thiamin, riboflavin, niacin, and vitamin B_6 all play important roles in maintaining healthy nerves, skin, hair, and eyes. Vitamin B_{12} is necessary for healthy cell production, but this vitamin is found only in foods of animal origin. Folic acid is vital to healthy cell production; in fact, too little folic acid in the diet can cause a type of anemia. Broccoli and the other cruciferous vegetables are good to excellent sources of the B vitamins except B_{12}.

Calcium

Calcium plays a key role in keeping bones and teeth healthy, and adequate amounts of this nutrient can help protect the body against the bone-thinning disease, osteoporosis. Broccoli and the other crucifers can make a substantial contribution toward the daily requirement.

Iron

Iron is necessary for the formation of healthy cells in the body. The iron contained in vegetables (nonheme iron) is less readily absorbed by the body than iron from meat sources (heme iron); however, the presence of vitamin C in a meal increases nonheme iron absorption. Since broccoli contains nearly four times the RDA for vitamin C, it can be considered a booster of nonheme iron absorption.

Potassium

Potassium helps maintain the fluid balance in all cells and is required for many of the enzyme reactions that take place in our body, such as nerve transmission, hormone secretion, and muscle contraction. Potassium is widely available in many foods, including the cruciferous vegetables.

Phosphorus

Phosphorus works with calcium and magnesium to ensure healthy bones; it's also needed for energy production. Broccoli is a good source of this necessary mineral.

Zinc

Zinc plays a role in wound healing and in maintaining a healthy immune system. The best sources for this mineral are meat, fish, and legumes; plant foods such as the crucifers contain relatively little zinc. However, many of the recipes in this book feature cruciferous vegetables in combination with meat, fish, or legumes, so you get the nutritional benefits of the crucifer *plus* other vital nutrients.

Magnesium

Like potassium, magnesium plays a role in nerve transmission and muscle function. This mineral also works in concert with calcium and phosphorus to maintain healthy bones. Broccoli is a very good source of magnesium.

Selenium

Selenium may help protect against heart disease and certain types of cancer. As with zinc, the best sources are meat and seafood. Following the recipes in this book which include meat or fish *and* vegetables can give you added protection against these diseases.

Sodium

Sodium is the chief regulator of the body's fluid balance. Most of us receive more than enough sodium in our diet, mainly from table salt (sodium chloride) and the high sodium content of many processed foods. The low sodium content of broccoli and the other crucifers make them perfect mainstays in everyone's diet—including those who must restrict sodium intake for health reasons.

The recipes in this book provide reduced-sodium alternatives to conventionally prepared, high-sodium ingredients such as chicken stock.

Convinced that the crucifers should be on *your* shopping list? Read on for tips on how to get the most nutrient power for your money when selecting, storing, and preparing these important vegetables.

TIPS TO RETAIN NUTRIENT POWER

Follow these tips for proper selection, storage, and preparation of the nutrient-rich crucifers.

"POWER" SHOPPING GUIDELINES

- Buy the freshest possible vegetables. First of all, they'll taste much better than vegetables that have been sitting around on supermarket shelves. Also, vitamin C is rapidly lost on exposure to oxygen; so if vegetables are damaged—even by a small breakage on a stalk, which often happens when they're on the shelf too long— they will lose some of their vitamin C content.

- Remember the old adage when selecting vegetables: the deeper the color, the more nutrients they're likely to contain.

- If you decide to buy frozen vegetables, purchase those packed in water instead of sauce. They're lower in fat and calories, and less expensive. Besides, you'll be seasoning them yourself as you follow the recipes in this book.

Selection Tips for Specific Crucifers

Broccoli: The freshest broccoli has a deep green color with a slightly purple hue. Look for tiny, tightly packed buds on the heads of broccoli and slender stems. Broccoli that has been in the store for a while will have open buds and thick, woody stems.

Brussels sprouts: These pungent-tasting vegetables look like tiny cabbages. Select sprouts that are firm and green; avoid yellow-looking sprouts with wilted leaves. In the fall, you can buy brussels sprouts on the stalk; these are your best bet for freshness.

Cabbage: There are many varieties of cabbage, including bok choy, or chinese cabbage, which is used in several of the recipes in this book. Select firm heads with a bright color—whether green, white, or red. Trim off the stalk and any discolored or limp outer leaves before using.

Cauliflower: Select firm, snowy white (or purple) heads with crisp green leaves at the base. Steer clear of heads mottled with brown spots or with limp, discolored leaves.

Kale: Select small, deep-green bunches of kale with clean, crisp leaves. Avoid large bunches with dry, browned, yellowed, or coarse-stemmed leaves.

Radishes: Select firm, bright red globes. Avoid those that are soft and discolored.

Turnips: There are three basic types of turnips: those with big yellow globes, called rutabagas; the familiar large white-globed turnips with green leaves on top; and tiny white-globed turnips. Select turnips with firm, waxy-looking bulbs and small green leaves.

"POWER" STORAGE TIPS

Since few of us shop daily for fresh vegetables, how you store the ones you buy is very important.

- Plan to use fresh fruits and vegetables as quickly as possible after purchase. You'll minimize storage time and maximize the nutrient content of your meal.

- If you cut up fresh vegetables to eat as a snack, store the pieces in an airtight container in the refrigerator or freezer.

- Store all vegetables—whole or cut up—in the refrigerator to retain nutrients as long as possible. Don't leave them out at room temperature.

- Never store vegetables in water, or they'll quickly lose all their vitamin C and folate—both of which dissolve in water.

"POWER" COOKING GUIDELINES

Vitamin C and the B vitamins are notoriously unstable in the presence of light, heat, and oxygen. To prevent vitamin loss during preparation and cooking, you'll need to take special care.

- Wash fresh vegetables, but don't soak them in water, or vitamins will leach out.

- Don't peel or cut them until you're ready to use them —again, because these vitamins disappear quickly when foods are exposed to the air.

- Steam or simmer vegetables in the smallest amount of water for the shortest amount of time possible (see How to Steam Broccoli to Crisp-Tender, p. 129), or stir-fry in a small amount of oil to lock in nutrients. *Never* boil.

Now turn the page to embark on a healthful adventure in the mouth-watering world of vegetable cookery!

SOUPS

LEMONY BROCCOLI RICE SOUP

This is a very delicate soup which is perfect for beginning a meal. Be sure to add the broccoli no more than 5 minutes before serving, or it will lose its bright green color.

Preparation time: 6 to 8 minutes
Cooking time: 20 minutes
Serves 4

4 cups chicken stock or reduced-sodium chicken broth
3 cloves garlic, minced
¹/₂ cup rice, uncooked
3 tablespoons lemon juice
1 teaspoon cornstarch
2 cups broccoli florets, broken into ¹/₄- to ¹/₂-inch florets
1 cup peeled and grated broccoli stems
¹/₂ cup very thinly sliced carrots
Salt to taste
Freshly ground black pepper, to taste
1 tablespoon Parmesan cheese, grated

1. In a large nonreactive saucepan, bring chicken stock to a boil. Add garlic and rice, lower heat, and simmer, covered, for 15 minutes.

2. Stir together lemon juice and cornstarch, add to stock, along with broccoli and carrots. Stir and cook until

rice is tender and vegetables are crisp-tender, about 5 minutes.

3. Remove from heat, season with salt and pepper. Ladle into serving bowls and sprinkle with Parmesan cheese.

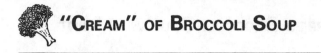

"CREAM" OF BROCCOLI SOUP

"Cream" does not necessarily mean high fat. This soup is rich and flavorful, without the extra calories.

Preparation time: 7 minutes
Cooking time: 10 to 15 minutes, depending on type of pasta used
Serves 4 to 5

 1 1/4 **pounds broccoli, chopped**
 1/2 **cup chopped onion**
 2 **cloves garlic, minced**
 1 **cup chopped celery**
 4 **cups water**
 1/2 **teaspoon salt**
 1/4 **teaspoon pepper**
 1/4 **cup pasta, any small shape (orzo, pastina, tubetti)**
 1/2 **cup chicken stock**
 1 **cup evaporated skim milk**
 Pinch nutmeg

1. In a large pot, simmer the first eight ingredients until pasta is tender. Cool slightly.

2. Purée with remaining ingredients (yes, the pasta too, it makes for a richer soup) until smooth. Serve.

CURRIED BROCCOLI SOUP WITH MINT

This is a lovely rich soup which is tasty and so easy to make. Serve it with sprigs of mint and a dollop of yogurt. It is also nice as a cold soup.

Preparation time: 8 minutes
Cooking time: 30 minutes
Serves 6

  2 tablespoons vegetable oil
  1 cup chopped onion
  2 cups chopped celery
  $2^1/_2$ tablespoons curry powder
  1 large bunch broccoli, cut into 2-inch pieces (about
    6 cups)
  2 cups chicken stock, reduced-sodium chicken broth,
    water, or a combination
  2 cups buttermilk
  4 teaspoons chopped fresh mint
  2 teaspoons lime juice
  Salt to taste
  Yogurt and mint for garnish

1. In a large saucepan, sauté onions and celery in oil over medium heat, until onions are soft. Add curry powder and stir until fragrant, about 1 minute.

2. Add broccoli and stock to pot and simmer, covered, until broccoli is very tender, 15 to 20 minutes. Remove from heat and cool slightly.

3. Place broccoli mixture, buttermilk, mint, lime juice, and salt in a food processor or blender and blend until smooth. Top with a dollop of yogurt and sprigs of mint. Serve.

HEARTY BROCCOLI VEGETABLE SOUP

Enjoy this soup with a thick slice of multigrain bread as a winter meal. Canned tomatoes can be substituted if ripe fresh ones are not available.

Preparation time: 15 minutes
Cooking time: 40 minutes
Serves 8 to 10

    3 tablespoons olive oil
    2 medium onions, chopped
    3 cloves garlic, minced
    3 large carrots, chopped
    3 celery stalks, chopped
    2 large potatoes, cut into ¹/₂-inch cubes
    2 cups broccoli stems, peeled and cut into ¹/₂-inch
      cubes
    1 teaspoon dried thyme
    1 bay leaf
    Freshly ground black pepper
    6 cups reduced-sodium chicken broth, reduced-
      sodium beef broth, water, or broth/water
      combination
    1 cup small pasta (pastina or tubetti)
    5 cups broccoli florets, broken into ¹/₂-inch pieces
    4 large tomatoes, peeled, seeded, and chopped
    2 cups white beans (navy, Great Northern, or small
      white), cooked according to package directions or
      canned (rinse and drain)
    Parsley for garnish

1. Heat oil in a heavy 8-quart pot, over medium heat. Add onions, garlic, carrots, and celery and cook, stirring constantly until onions become translucent.

2. Add potatoes, broccoli stems, thyme, bay leaf, black pepper, and broth or water.

3. Bring to a boil, reduce heat, and simmer for 25 minutes. Add pasta and cook for another 5 minutes.

4. Add remaining ingredients. Bring soup to a boil, reduce heat, and simmer for 5 minutes.

5. Remove from heat and cool for 5 minutes. Season with salt and pepper. Serve in bowls, sprinkled with chopped fresh parsley.

SWEET AND PUNGENT CABBAGE SOUP

This is a wonderful winter vegetable soup. The sweet and pungent flavors are fabulous and it has a nice rustic look.

Preparation time: 10 minutes
Cooking time: 45 minutes
Serves 6 to 8

6 cups chopped cabbage
1 teaspoon minced garlic
1¹/₂ cups chopped onion
1¹/₂ cups chopped carrots
1 cup chopped celery
1 teaspoon grated orange zest
¹/₃ cup tomato paste
¹/₄ cup vinegar
1 tablespoon sugar
1 bay leaf
6 cups water, chicken or beef stock, reduced-sodium chicken or beef broth, or a water/stock combination
1¹/₂ teaspoons salt, or to taste
¹/₂ teaspoon freshly ground black pepper, or to taste

1. Place cabbage, garlic, onion, carrots, celery, orange zest, tomato paste, vinegar, sugar, bay leaf, and water or stock in a large, heavy-bottomed saucepan. Bring to a boil, lower heat, and simmer, partially covered, until vegetables are very tender, 45 minutes.

2. Season with salt and pepper and serve.

BROCCOLI, LEEK, AND
WATERCRESS SOUP

Four delicious flavors combine beautifully to make one
smooth soup. Enjoy the simple combination.

Preparation time: 15 minutes
Cooking time: 20 minutes
Serves 6 to 8

1 tablespoon olive oil
1 cup chopped onion
2 cups leeks, (about 1/3 lb.) cleaned well and
    chopped
4 cups chicken stock, or reduced-sodium chicken
    broth
2 cups potatoes, cut into 1/2-inch cubes
2 cups chopped broccoli florets
2 cups peeled and chopped broccoli stems
1 cup broccoli florets broken into 1/2-inch pieces
2 cups watercress leaves, packed down

1. Heat oil in a large, heavy-bottomed saucepan, over medium-low heat. Add onion and chopped leeks and
   cook until tender, about 5 minutes.

2. Add chicken stock, potatoes, chopped broccoli florets
   and stems. Cover and simmer until potatoes are
   cooked and broccoli is tender. Meanwhile, steam remaining broken florets to crisp-tender (instructions,
   see p. 129) and set aside.

3. Add watercress leaves to potato, broccoli, and leek mixture and cook until wilted. Cool slightly. Purée mixture in a food processor or blender until smooth. Serve with steamed florets on top.

 # CHINESE CABBAGE SOUP

This soup has a very delicate, yet very authentic flavor. It is easy to make and a perfect way to prepare the palate for the forthcoming meal.

Preparation time: 10 minutes
Cooking time: 5 minutes
Serves 4

> **4 cups chicken stock or reduced-sodium chicken broth**
> **3 cups bok choy (chinese cabbage) cut in $^1/_2$-inch by 3-inch pieces**
> **$^1/_2$ cup very thin 2-inch carrot straws**
> **$^1/_2$ cup straw mushrooms**
> **4 strips lemon peel, $^1/_2$ inch by 2 inches**
> **4 strips lime peel, $^1/_2$ inch by 2 inches**
> **4 strips orange peel, $^1/_2$ inch by 2 inches**
> **1 tablespoon thinly sliced scallions**
> **Oriental sesame oil**

1. In a large pot, heat broth to boiling, lower heat to simmer, and add bok choy. Cook until bok choy is almost crisp-tender (instructions, see p. 129). Add carrots and mushrooms and cook 1 minute.

2. In each of four serving bowls, place a strip each of lemon, lime, and orange peel. Pour hot soup over peels, sprinkle with scallions and a few drops of sesame oil, and serve.

SALADS

Broccoli and Fennel Salad

I love fennel! Its crisp, distinctive flavor is a smashing match for the king of the cabbage family.

Preparation time: 10 minutes
Cooking time: None
Serves 4 to 6

> ³/₄ **pound broccoli, broken into** ¹/₂**-inch florets, stems peeled and cut in strips** ¹/₄**-inch wide, steamed to crisp-tender (instructions, see p. 129)**
> ¹/₂ **pound head fennel, cut into thin strips**
> ¹/₂ **cup red bell pepper, cut into thin strips**
> ¹/₄ **cup black olives, pitted and cut into slivers**
> **2 tablespoons chopped fresh basil**
> **1**¹/₂ **tablespoons dijon mustard**
> **2 tablespoons white wine vinegar**
> **2 tablespoons lemon juice**
> **2 cloves garlic, minced**
> **2 tablespoons water**
> ¹/₂ **teaspoon pepper**
> ¹/₄ **teaspoon salt, or to taste**
> **1 tablespoon olive oil**

1. In a large bowl, combine broccoli, fennel, red pepper, olives, and basil.

2. In a separate bowl, whisk together remaining ingredients. Toss with broccoli mixture and serve.

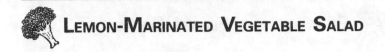 LEMON-MARINATED VEGETABLE SALAD

This refreshing dish makes a lovely addition to a summer meal, but I prepare it year round. The crunchy vegetables and lemony zing make it a festive treat.

Preparation time: 10 minutes, plus 1 hour or more to marinate
Cooking time: None
Serves 6

- **2 tablespoons olive oil**
- **3 tablespoons lemon juice**
- **^{1}/₄ cup chopped fresh dill**
- **^{1}/₂ teaspoon freshly ground black pepper, or to taste**
- **^{1}/₂ teaspoon salt, or to taste**
- **1^1/₂ pounds broccoli, broken into ^{1}/₂-inch florets, stalks peeled and sliced lengthwise into ^{1}/₄-inch slices, steamed to crisp-tender (instructions, see p. 129)**
- **2 carrots, sliced ^{1}/₈-inch thick, about 1 to 1^1/₂ cups**
- **4 scallions, including 4 inches of green, thinly sliced**
- **1^1/₂ cups jicama, cut in ^{1}/₄-inch by 2-inch sticks (if available)**
- **4 cups romaine lettuce, cut crosswise into strips ^{1}/₂ inch wide**

1. In a large nonmetal bowl, combine oil, lemon juice, dill, pepper, and salt. Add broccoli, carrots, scallions, and jicama and toss well.

2. Cover and refrigerate, stirring once after $1/2$ hour, for at least 1 hour.

3. Toss with lettuce and serve promptly.

SOUTHWESTERN BROCCOLI SALAD

I love the flavors in this salad, but the colors are what really make it special. Try serving it with grilled marinated chicken, either on the side or tossed into the salad.

Preparation time: 10 minutes
Cooking time: 1 minute
Serves 4

> **3 cups broccoli, broken into $^1/_2$-inch florets, stems peeled and cut in $^1/_4$-inch by 1-inch sticks, steamed to crisp-tender (instructions, see p. 129)**
> $^1/_2$ **cup shredded carrots**
> $^1/_2$ **cup corn kernels, cooked**
> $^1/_2$ **cup black beans, canned or cooked (rinse and drain, if canned)**
> $^1/_4$ **cup chopped red onion**
> **2 tablespoons chopped cilantro**
> $^3/_4$ **teaspoon cumin**
> $^1/_2$ **teaspoon finely chopped jalapeño**
> **1 tablespoon lime juice**
> **4 teaspoons olive oil**

1. Combine broccoli, carrots, corn, black beans, onion, and cilantro in a large bowl.

2. In a small saucepan, heat cumin over low heat just until fragrant, about 1 minute. Stir together with jalapeño, lime juice, and olive oil. Pour over vegetables and toss. Serve.

RED CABBAGE SALAD WITH GINGER DRESSING

The colors in this salad are breathtaking, but it is not only beautiful to look at. Be sure to make it a couple of hours ahead to allow the flavors to soak into the vegetables.

Preparation time: 5 minutes
Cooking time: 1 minute
Serves 6

$^1/_4$ **pound snow peas, ends snipped**
1 pound red cabbage, thinly shredded
1 yellow pepper, cut in $^1/_4$-inch strips
1 red pepper, cut in $^1/_4$-inch strips
2 tablespoon grated ginger
$^1/_2$ **teaspoon soy sauce**
1 tablespoon rice wine vinegar or apple cider vinegar
2 tablespoons vegetable oil
2 strips lemon zest $^1/_2$ inch by 1 inch, cut in thin slivers
2 tablespoons thinly sliced scallion tops, green part only

1. Cook snow peas in a pot of boiling water until bright green, 15 to 30 seconds. Drain and quickly rinse under cold water until cool. Combine with cabbage and peppers.

(*Continued on next page*)

2. With a hand mixer or wire whisk, beat together ginger, soy sauce, and vinegar. Add vegetable oil in a thin stream, while beating vigorously.

3. Toss together cabbage mixture, ginger dressing, lemon zest, and scallion tops. Refrigerate for at least 1 hour before serving.

DIFFERENT COLE SLAW

Here is a lighter version of the classic. I much prefer it to the mayonnaise-soaked recipe of the past.

Preparation time: 10 minutes
Cooking time: None
Serves 6

4 cups thinly shredded green cabbage
1 cup grated carrots
1¹/₂ ribs celery, sliced lengthwise into thin sticks
    (1 cup)
¹/₂ cup thinly sliced red onion
2 teaspoons celery seeds
4 teaspoons dijon mustard
4 teaspoons cider vinegar
2 teaspoons sugar
1 tablespoon vegetable oil
¹/₂ cup plain low-fat yogurt

1. In a large bowl, combine cabbage, carrots, celery, and red onion. Set aside.

2. Stir together remaining ingredients and toss with cabbage mixture. Serve.

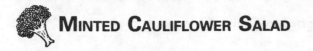

MINTED CAULIFLOWER SALAD

Cauliflower and mint is a flavor combination that astounded me when I tasted a similar recipe by Shirley King, a brilliant chef and teacher of mine. She also taught me that cooking cauliflower in milk helps to keep it white, but you can steam it if you don't care about the color.

Preparation time: 3 minutes
Cooking time: 8 to 10 minutes
Serves 4

> **4 cups water**
> **1 cup milk**
> **1 medium head cauliflower, cut into 1-inch florets**
> **2 tablespoons light olive oil**
> **1 tablespoon white vinegar**
> **¹/₄ teaspoon dijon mustard**
> **pinch salt**
> **2 tablespoons chopped fresh mint**
> **1 tablespoon thinly sliced scallions**

1. In a large pot, bring water and milk to a boil. Place florets in water and boil gently until crisp-tender, 8 to 10 minutes. Drain.

2. Combine remaining ingredients. Add warm cauliflower, toss, cool, and serve.

SPICY MARINATED BROCCOLI

If you like spice, you will love this. Broccoli stands up beautifully to powerful flavors . . . and this is a doozy! The broccoli is just barely cooked in the marinade, as it cools.

Preparation time: 3 minutes, plus time to marinate
Cooking time: 4 minutes
Serves 2

> 5 cloves garlic, minced
> $^1/_4$ cup tomato paste
> $^1/_2$ teaspoon hot red pepper flakes
> 1 teaspoon chopped lemon peel
> 3 tablespoons lime juice
> 1 cup water
> 1 pound broccoli, florets broken into $1^1/_2$-inch
>   pieces, stems peeled and cut into sticks $^1/_4$ inch
>   wide

1. In a small saucepan, combine first six ingredients and heat to boiling. Cook for 3 minutes. Remove from heat. Add broccoli to the saucepan and transfer to a medium bowl or container.

2. Cool and refrigerate mixture for 2 or more hours before serving.

BROCCOLI TOMATO VINAIGRETTE

This dish is best in summer when the tomatoes are sweet and ruby red and fresh basil is everywhere. Try tossing it with some cooked rice for a more substantial salad.

Preparation time: 7 minutes
Cooking time: None
Serves 6

1 1/2 pounds broccoli, broken into 1-inch florets, stems peeled, split lengthwise and sliced 1/4-inch thick, steamed to crisp-tender (instructions, see p. 129)
1/2 cup thinly sliced red onion
1 pound tomatoes, cut in 1-inch wedges
1/4 cup red wine vinegar
1/4 teaspoon mustard
3 tablespoons olive oil
1/2 teaspoon freshly ground black pepper
1 teaspoon salt
1/2 teaspoon sugar
1/3 cup shredded fresh basil leaves, tightly packed

1. In a large bowl, combine broccoli, onion, and tomatoes.

2. Whisk together vinegar, mustard, oil, pepper, salt, and sugar. Pour over vegetables, add basil, and toss. Serve.

BRUSSELS SPROUTS WITH ORANGE AND WALNUTS

When brussels sprouts are separated into leaves, the flavor is so delicate. The leaves are beautifully complimented by fresh fruit and this simple, bright-flavored dressing.

Preparation time: 3 minutes
Cooking time: 2 to 3 minutes
Serves 4 to 6

2 10-ounce packages brussels sprouts
2 tablespoons olive oil
$^1/_3$ cup orange juice
$^3/_4$ teaspoon salt
4 oranges, peeled with a knife and separated into segments; discard membrane
$^1/_4$ cup chopped walnuts, lightly toasted

1. Separate brussels sprout leaves by slicing off stem end of sprout, removing bottom leaves, slicing again and peeling off leaves. Continue until all the leaves are separated. Steam leaves over gently boiling water until bright green, 2 to 3 minutes. Rinse with cold water to cool. Drain well.

2. Whisk together oil, juice, and salt. Toss with brussels sprout leaves, orange segments, and nuts. Serve.

BROCCOLI STEMS AND FRUIT SALAD

It may sound like an odd combination, but broccoli stems have a lively crisp freshness that blends perfectly with fruit. Add any fruits that you like!

Preparation time: 10 minutes
Cooking time: None
Serves 4

  $^1/_4$ cup orange juice
  $^1/_4$ cup lime juice
  1 tablespoon chopped fresh mint leaves
  3 cups peeled and diced ($^1/_4$-inch cubes) broccoli
    stems (2 bunches)
  1$^1/_2$ cups diced ($^1/_4$-inch cubes) green apple
  1 cup halved or quartered strawberries
  1 cup halved red grapes

In a bowl, combine all ingredients and mix thoroughly. Serve.

BRUSSELS SPROUTS AND CAULIFLOWER WITH CURRIED YOGURT

The dressing on this salad is so flavorful, it can be served on almost any vegetable. If you want to use only the brussels sprouts or cauliflower, feel free.

Preparation time: 15 minutes
Cooking time: None
Serves 6

2 teaspoons vegetable oil
2 tablespoons curry powder
$^1/_4$ teaspoon ground cloves
$^1/_4$ teaspoon ground coriander
$^1/_4$ cup water
$^1/_2$ cup plain low-fat yogurt
$^1/_2$ teaspoon salt
$^1/_2$ teaspoon sugar
1 Granny Smith apple, cored and cut into
   bite-size chunks
$^1/_2$ cup golden raisins
1 to 1$^1/_4$ pounds cauliflower, cut into bite-size
   pieces, steamed to crisp-tender
6 ounces brussels sprouts, cut in half lengthwise
   and steamed to crisp-tender

For crisp-tender steaming of vegetables, see page 129.

(*Continued on next page*)

1. Combine oil, curry powder, cloves, coriander, and water in a small saucepan over medium-low heat. Stir mixture constantly until thick. Cool slightly.

2. Add curry mixture to yogurt, salt, and sugar. Toss with remaining ingredients. Serve.

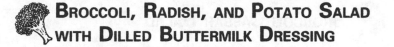 # BROCCOLI, RADISH, AND POTATO SALAD WITH DILLED BUTTERMILK DRESSING

This salad combines the fresh flavor of dill, the crunch of broccoli, and the smoothness of potato with the zestiness of another cruciferous vegetable—the radish. Don't forget to give the buttermilk and dill some time to combine.

Preparation time: 8 to 10 minutes
Cooking time: None
Serves 4

$^1/_2$ **cup buttermilk**
$^1/_4$ **cup chopped fresh dill**
$^1/_2$ **teaspoon salt**
Pinch white pepper
1 pound broccoli, broken into $^1/_2$-inch florets, stems
    peeled and cut into $^1/_2$-inch cubes (3 cups)
1$^1/_2$ cups peeled, cubed, cooked potato
1 cup radishes, cut in $^1/_4$-inch wedges

1. In a bowl, combine buttermilk, dill, salt and pepper. Stir and refrigerate for at least 1 hour.

2. Combine remaining ingredients and toss with dressing. Serve.

 **BROCCOLI CAESAR SALAD**

Broccoli with Caesar dressing is a fabulous combination. This is a light version of the classic, tossed with broccoli and tomatoes. Add any other vegetables that you like.

Preparation time: 8 minutes
Cooking time: None
Serves 4

> **3 cups (1 bunch) broccoli florets broken into 1-inch pieces, steamed to crisp-tender (instructions, see p. 129)**
> **1 cup halved cherry tomatoes**
> **$^1/_2$ cup buttermilk**
> **2 tablespoons grated Parmesan cheese**
> **1 teaspoon chopped anchovies**
> **1 clove garlic, minced**
> **$^1/_4$ teaspoon freshly ground black pepper**
> **$^1/_4$ teaspoon mustard powder**
> **1 tablespoon part-skim or nonfat ricotta cheese**
> **1 tablespoon chopped parsley**

1. In a bowl, combine broccoli and tomatoes. Set aside.

2. In a blender or food processor, mix buttermilk, Parmesan cheese, anchovies, garlic, pepper, and mustard powder.

3. Stir ricotta and parsley into dressing and toss with broccoli and tomatoes. Serve.

BROCCOLI BARLEY SALAD PROVENCALE

This is a hearty salad with flavors reminiscent of the South of France. Served on a bed of greens, it can be enjoyed as a meal on its own.

Preparation time: 15 minutes
Cooking time: None
Serves 4 to 6

1 cup barley, cooked (about 3 cups)
1 1/2 pounds broccoli, cut into 1/2-inch florets, stems
    peeled and cut into 1/4-inch cubes, steamed to
    crisp-tender (instructions, see p. 129)
1/2 cup diced carrots
1/2 cup diced radishes
1 tablespoon olive oil
2 tablespoons chopped olives
1 clove garlic, minced
2 teaspoons red wine vinegar
2 teaspoons fresh or 1/2 teaspoon dried thyme
1 teaspoon salt
1/2 teaspoon freshly ground black pepper

In a large bowl, combine all ingredients. Mix well. Serve.

BROCCOLI BROWN RICE SALAD WITH YOGURT DRESSING

This is a salad that my friend Liza makes when she wants to prepare something really healthful. Make the rice and dressing a day ahead and it becomes a very quick meal.

Preparation time: 10 minutes, plus 2 hours for dressing to blend
Cooking time: None
Serves 4

1 cup plain low-fat yogurt
$^1/_4$ cup chopped parsley
1 teaspoon fresh tarragon, or $^1/_2$ teaspoon dried
1 clove garlic, minced
1 tablespoon lemon juice
1 teaspoon honey
2 teaspoons soy sauce
Freshly ground black pepper, to taste
3 cups cooked brown rice
1$^1/_4$ pounds broccoli (about 4 cups), florets broken into $^3/_4$-inch pieces, stems peeled and cut into $^1/_4$-inch by 1$^1/_2$-inch sticks, steamed to crisp-tender (instructions, see p. 129)
$^1/_4$ cup seeded and diced tomato
$^1/_4$ cup diced red onion
$^1/_4$ cup chick-peas
1 cup cucumber, cut into $^1/_4$-inch by 1$^1/_2$-inch sticks
1 teaspoon olive oil
2 tablespoons broken cashews

1. In a nonmetal bowl, combine yogurt, parsley, tarragon, garlic, lemon juice, honey, soy sauce, and pepper. Cover and refrigerate for 2 or more hours.

2. Combine rice, broccoli, tomato, onion, chick-peas, cucumber, oil, and cashews in a bowl. Toss together to combine.

3. Divide salad mixture onto 4 plates, make a well in the center of each. Fill with yogurt dressing. Serve.

BROCCOLI AND LENTIL SALAD

This is a very substantial salad and can also be served warm, as a side dish. Be sure not to overcook the lentils— different varieties will take different amounts of time.

Preparation time: 5 minutes
Cooking time: 20 to 30 minutes
Serves 6

- 1 cup lentils
- 2 tablespoons chopped parsley
- 2 teaspoons fresh sage, or 1 teaspoon dried, chopped with parsley
- 2 tablespoons olive oil
- 1 tablespoon red wine vinegar
- $^1/_4$ teaspoon salt
- $1^1/_4$ pounds broccoli (about 4 cups), florets only, cut into $^1/_2$-inch pieces, steamed to crisp-tender (instructions, see p. 129)
- $^1/_3$ cup sweet white onion, chopped
- $^1/_4$ large red bell pepper, chopped

1. In a large saucepan, cook lentils in 6 cups water. Bring water and lentils to a boil, lower heat, and simmer, uncovered, until lentils are just tender, 20 to 30 minutes. Drain.

2. Whisk together parsley, sage, oil, vinegar, and salt. Toss with lentils and remaining ingredients, cool and serve.

MAIN COURSES

Chicken and Vegetable Stir-Fry

It's easy to forget how healthful Chinese food can be. Here is a light, fast, and delicious dinner—with an Asian twang!

Preparation time: 10 minutes, plus 30 minutes to marinate
Cooking time: 10 minutes
Serves 4

- 1 pound boneless chicken breasts, cut in ¹/₂-inch by 2-inch strips
- 2 tablespoons lemon juice
- 2 tablespoons grated or finely chopped fresh ginger
- 1 tablespoon reduced-sodium soy sauce
- 1 tablespoon Oriental sesame oil (if unavailable, use vegetable oil)
- 2 cloves garlic, minced
- 1 teaspoon hot pepper flakes (optional)
- 2 tablespoons vegetable oil
- ¹/₄ cup chicken stock
- 1 teaspoon cornstarch
- 1¹/₄ pounds broccoli, broken into bite-size florets, stems peeled and cut into diagonal ¹/₄-inch slices, steamed to crisp-tender (instructions, see p. 129)
- 2 red peppers, cut into 1-inch squares
- 2 cups diagonally sliced celery
- 1 medium onion, cut into 1-inch squares

1. In a large nonmetal bowl, marinate chicken in lemon juice, ginger, soy sauce, sesame oil, garlic, and hot pepper for 30 minutes.

2. Heat vegetable oil in a large skillet or wok over high heat. When oil is very hot, add chicken pieces (reserve marinade). Cook on one side for 2 minutes. Turn and cook chicken thoroughly (about 2 minutes). Remove from pan.

3. Combine reserved marinade, chicken stock, and cornstarch.

4. Reheat pan. Add vegetables and cook, stirring frequently, until onions have wilted. Add marinade/stock mixture to pan and stir until boiling. Lower heat and simmer for 1 minute or until sauce has thickened.

5. Add cooked chicken pieces and toss with vegetables and sauce. Serve with rice.

SWEET AND SOUR CHICKEN AND BROCCOLI

Serve this classic Chinese-American dish with lots of brown rice. The sauce is sweetened naturally with pineapple juice and a touch of honey.

Preparation time: 10 minutes
Cooking time: 10 to 12 minutes
Serves 4

2 teaspoons vegetable oil
³/₄ pound boneless chicken breasts, cut into 1-inch cubes
¹/₄ cup thinly sliced scallions
¹/₄ cup finely diced green bell pepper
¹/₂ cup finely diced red bell pepper
³/₄ cup pineapple juice
3 tablespoons apple cider vinegar
1 teaspoon grated ginger
¹/₂ teaspoon grated lemon zest
1 teaspoon honey
1 teaspoon soy sauce
¹/₂ teaspoon ground coriander
Pinch white pepper
¹/₄ cup chicken stock or reduced-sodium chicken broth
2 tablespoons white wine
³/₄ teaspoon cornstarch
1 pound broccoli, cut into 1-inch florets, steamed to crisp-tender (instructions, see p. 129)

1. Heat oil in a nonstick skillet over medium-high heat. Add chicken pieces and cook, stirring until golden. Cover and cook thoroughly. Remove and set aside.

2. Add scallions and peppers and cook until lightly browned. Add pineapple juice, vinegar, ginger, lemon zest, honey, soy sauce, coriander, and white pepper. Heat to boiling.

3. Combine stock, wine, and cornstarch. Add to skillet, stirring constantly until sauce is thick and clear. Return chicken to skillet, add broccoli, and coat with sauce. Serve with rice.

BROCCOLI WITH BEEF AND ORANGE SAUCE

This dish is irresistible. The meat is so tender and the sauce so tangy and delicious . . . just perfect for broccoli!

Preparation time: 10 minutes, plus 30 minutes to marinate
Cooking time: 7 to 8 minutes
Serves 4

$3/4$ pound flank steak, cut into $3/4$-inch cubes
Peel of 1 orange, cut in long, very thin strips
1 tablespoon cornstarch
1 tablespoon soy sauce
1 teaspoon sugar
$1/2$ teaspoon baking soda
1 tablespoon water
1 tablespoon vegetable oil
1 pound broccoli, cut in 1-inch florets, stems peeled
  and cut in $1/4$-inch diagonal slices
2 medium carrots, cut in $1/4$-inch diagonal slices
  (about 1 cup)
$1/2$ cup sherry
Pinch sugar
Pinch salt
1 teaspoon vegetable oil
2 tablespoons sliced scallions
1 tablespoon beef stock, or reduced-sodium broth or
  water
2 tablespoons orange juice concentrate
1 teaspoon soy sauce

$^1/_2$ teaspoon cornstarch
$^1/_4$ teaspoon cayenne pepper

1. In a large bowl, mix together first seven ingredients and marinate for at least 30 minutes.

2. In a large nonstick skillet or wok, heat 1 tablespoon of oil over high heat until very hot. Add beef and orange rinds to oil and cook, stirring, until beef pieces just turn white, about 1 minute. Remove beef and rinds and set aside.

3. Place broccoli, carrots, sherry, sugar, and salt in skillet and cook, stirring, until broccoli is crisp-tender, 3 to 4 minutes. Remove broccoli and carrots from skillet.

4. Stir together remaining ingredients. Pour into skillet, stirring. Return beef and orange rind to skillet and toss with sauce, until sauce thickens and coats beef. Pour over broccoli and carrots and serve.

PORK MEDALLIONS WITH BALSAMIC HERB SAUCE AND BROCCOLI

Balsamic vinegar is fantastic with pork and broccoli, but feel free to leave out the pork. Make the sauce and serve it over steamed broccoli for a great side dish.

Preparation time: 5 minutes
Cooking time: 15 minutes
Serves 4

   2 teaspoons olive oil
   1 pound pork tenderloin, cut into thin medallions
   2 tablespoons chopped shallots
   $^1/_4$ cup balsamic vinegar
   $^1/_2$ cup plus 3 tablespoons chicken stock or reduced-sodium chicken broth
   $^1/_2$ teaspoon fresh or $^1/_4$ teaspoon dried thyme
   $^1/_2$ teaspoon cornstarch
   3 cups or (1 bunch) broccoli florets, broken into 1-inch pieces, steamed to crisp-tender (instructions, see p. 129)

1. Heat oil in a nonstick skillet over medium-high heat. Add pork and sear on each side until golden and just cooked through, 1 to 2 minutes per side. Remove pork from pan, blot medallions with paper towels and set aside.

2. Add shallots to skillet and cook, stirring constantly until soft, about 1 minute. Add vinegar, 3 tablespoons broth, and thyme. Increase heat and boil, stirring occa-

sionally, until vinegar fragrance subsides, 3 to 5 minutes.

3. Add remaining chicken broth and cornstarch and cook sauce, stirring constantly, until it thickens, about 8 minutes. Remove from heat, toss with broccoli and serve atop pork medallions.

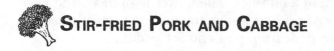

STIR-FRIED PORK AND CABBAGE

Pork and cabbage are the ingredients in moo shu pork, but this recipe gives you an opportunity to taste the flavors. Try serving it like moo shu pork by rolling it up in lettuce leaves with a bit of hoisin sauce.

Preparation time: 8 minutes
Cooking time: 8 to 10 minutes
Serves 4

$^1/_2$ **pound pork loin, cut into very thin slivers across the grain**
2 **teaspoons reduced-sodium soy sauce**
2 **teaspoons dry sherry**
1 **egg white**
1 **teaspoon cornstarch**
2 **teaspoons vegetable oil**
1 **clove garlic, minced**
1 **2-inch piece ginger, cut in very thin slivers**
1 **medium onion, cut in thin rings**
8 **cups shredded green cabbage**
1 **cup shredded carrots**
2 **tablespoons reduced-sodium soy sauce**
$^1/_4$ **cup sherry**

1. In a bowl, toss pork with 2 teaspoons soy sauce and 2 teaspoons sherry. Leave for 1 minute. Add egg white to coat meat. Strain off excess egg white and toss meat with cornstarch.

2. Heat oil in a nonstick skillet, over high heat. Add pork and cook, stirring frequently until it begins to brown. Remove pork from pan and set aside.

3. Add garlic, ginger, onion, and cabbage to skillet and cook, stirring, until cabbage is well coated. Cover until cabbage is wilted, 1 to 2 minutes. Add remaining ingredients and cooked pork to skillet. Cook until liquid is absorbed. Serve.

SHRIMP WITH GINGER, APPLES, AND BROCCOLI STEMS

The flavors of this dish are so fresh! I like to serve it with brown rice and a glass of beer.

Preparation time: 10 minutes
Cooking time: 10 minutes
Serves 4

> 1 tablespoon vegetable oil
> 1 Granny Smith apple, peeled and cut into 16
>   wedges
> $^1/_2$ cup apple juice
> 3 tablespoons cider vinegar
> 1 teaspoon cornstarch
> 2 tablespoons chopped shallots
> 1 teaspoon grated ginger
> 3 cups broccoli stems, peeled and cut into $^1/_4$-inch
>   diagonal slices
> 1 pound shrimp, peeled and deveined
> Salt to taste
> Freshly ground black pepper to taste
> 1 tablespoon finely shredded fresh basil leaves

1. Heat oil in a large nonstick skillet, over medium heat. Add apple pieces and cook, turning occasionally until lightly browned. Remove and set aside.

2. In a small bowl stir together apple juice, vinegar, and cornstarch. Set aside.

3. In the same skillet, cook shallots and ginger until shallots are wilted. Add broccoli and apple and cider mixture and toss. Cook, stirring occasionally until sauce begins to thicken.

4. Add shrimp and cook until pink. Season with salt and pepper. Sprinkle with basil strips and serve.

RED CABBAGE, TURKEY SAUSAGE, AND POTATO HASH

This is a really nice hearty dish to serve in the winter. It has a lovely combination of sweet, pungent, and garlicky tastes.

Preparation time: 10 minutes
Cooking time: 16 to 18 minutes
Serves 4

$^3/_4$ pound turkey sausage, removed from casing
1 head red cabbage, cut in 1-inch squares
$^1/_4$ teaspoon thyme
$^1/_2$ teaspoon fennel seeds
$^1/_4$ cup vinegar
$^1/_2$ cup apple juice
$^1/_4$ teaspoon salt
Pinch sugar
2 medium potatoes, peeled, cooked, and cut in $^1/_2$-inch cubes (about 2 cups)
1 cup coarsely chopped Granny Smith apple
$2^1/_2$ cups thinly sliced onions
3 cloves garlic, minced

1. Brown sausage, breaking it into small pieces, in a large nonstick skillet. When browned, remove from skillet, pour off grease and wipe skillet with a paper towel.

2. Place cabbage, thyme, fennel seeds, vinegar, apple juice, salt, and sugar in the skillet. Cover and cook until cabbage is wilted. Remove cabbage mixture from skillet and set aside.

3. Return sausage to skillet, add potatoes, apples, onions, and garlic. Cook mixture until onions and potatoes are golden. Return cabbage mixture to skillet, mix well and continue cooking until heated through. Serve.

"DIVINE" CHICKEN AND BROCCOLI

Here is a light version of Chicken Divan. Instead of a heavy mornay sauce, I use low-fat milk and chicken stock. It is much lighter but still very tasty.

Preparation time: 25 minutes
Cooking time: 25 to 35 minutes
Serves 4

>   1 red bell pepper, roasted
>   1 pound skinless chicken meat, cooked and cut into strips
>   4 cups (1 large bunch) broccoli florets, broken into 1-inch pieces, steamed to crisp-tender (instructions, p. 129)
>   2 cups chicken stock or reduced-sodium broth
>   1 cup low-fat milk
>   3 tablespoons vegetable oil
>   3 tablespoons flour
> $1/4$ cup grated Parmesan cheese
> $1/4$ teaspoon white pepper
>   2 teaspoons Worcestershire sauce
>   Bread crumbs for topping

1. Prepare roasted red pepper (see below).

2. Preheat oven to 400°F. Layer chicken and broccoli in a baking dish. Set aside.

3. In a saucepan, heat chicken stock and milk to just simmering. In another saucepan, heat oil over medium-

low heat. Add flour and cook, stirring constantly with a whisk, until mixture is thick and golden, about 3 minutes.

4. Slowly add stock and milk, whisking constantly, removing any lumps that form. Continue cooking and whisking, over low heat, until thick, about 10 minutes.

5. Stir in cheese, white pepper, and Worcestershire sauce. Pour sauce over layered chicken and broccoli, sprinkle on bread crumbs, and arrange roasted red pepper strips on top.

6. Bake until sauce is bubbling, 25 to 35 minutes. Serve.

How to Roast Red Peppers

1. Quarter peppers, core, and arrange on an aluminum foil-lined baking sheet, skin side up. Place under broiler, 2 or 3 inches from heat source. Roast until skins of peppers are evenly blackened, about 12 minutes.

2. Close aluminum foil around peppers, to prevent steam from escaping. Allow peppers to cool in foil, about 10 minutes.

 OVEN-ROASTED FISH AND BROCCOLI CASSEROLE

This might just be the perfect recipe. It is delicious, healthful, and easy to make. You can assemble the casserole hours ahead, but be sure not to use a metal pan—the lemon will react and make it funny-tasting.

Preparation time: 10 minutes
Cooking time: 20 to 25 minutes
Serves 4

1¼ pounds broccoli, broken into 2-inch florets,
   stems peeled and cut into ½-inch diagonal slices
2 medium onions, very thinly sliced
2 carrots, peeled and cut in thin diagonal slices
1 lemon, thinly sliced
2 tablespoons olive oil
½ teaspoon white pepper
1 teaspoon cumin
1½ pounds cod, salmon, or other large fish fillet,
   cut in strips 1-inch wide
½ cup chopped parsley
¼ cup lemon juice

1. Preheat oven to 450°F.

2. In a bowl, toss together broccoli, onions, carrots, lemon, oil, pepper, and cumin. Place in a baking dish and cook until onions are wilted, about 8 minutes.

(Continued on next page)

3. Add fish, parsley, and lemon juice to baking dish and toss to coat fish with onion mixture. Cover dish with aluminum foil and bake until fish is cooked through, about 10 to 15 minutes. Serve.

FARMER'S PIE

When I was little, I loved shepherd's pie made with ground beef and canned alphabet soup. Now I make this vegetable-based version, but I do miss the tiny ABC's.

Preparation time: 10 minutes
Cooking time: 50 to 55 minutes
Serves 4

1 teaspoon vegetable oil
1 cup chopped onion
³/₄ pound ground turkey
2 carrots, sliced ¹/₄-inch thick
1 small rib celery, sliced ¹/₄-inch thick
2 cups sliced mushrooms
1 pound broccoli, broken into 1-inch florets, stems
   peeled and cut into ¹/₄-inch diagonal slices
2¹/₄ cups chicken stock, or reduced-sodium chicken
   broth
2¹/₂ teaspoons fresh or 1¹/₄ teaspoons dried
   rosemary
1 teaspoon fresh or ¹/₂ teaspoon dried thyme
3 tablespoons sun-dried tomatoes, chopped
1 tablespoon cornstarch
2 or 3 large Idaho potatoes, peeled, cooked, and
   mashed with 2 tsp. butter and ¹/₃ cup lowfat milk
   (3 cups)

(*Continued on next page*)

1. Preheat oven to 375°F.

2. In a skillet, cook onions in oil until transparent, add turkey, and continue to cook until it just begins to brown. Add carrots, celery, and mushrooms and continue cooking, stirring until well combined. Add broccoli.

3. Pour 2 cups of stock over turkey/vegetable mixture, add herbs and tomatoes and bring to a simmer. Stir together remaining stock and cornstarch, and add to turkey and vegetable mixture quickly, stirring continuously. Continue cooking and stirring until sauce has thickened, 8 to 10 minutes.

4. Pour into a 6-cup baking dish and spoon mashed potatoes over top of mixture, covering completely. Bake until top is golden, about 45 minutes. Serve.

MIDDLE EASTERN CHICKEN PILAF WITH CAULIFLOWER AND ALMONDS

This is a wonderful one-dish meal. The sweet and spicy flavors make for an exotic dish that even children will like.

Preparation time: 10 minutes
Cooking time: 1 hour, 15 minutes
Serves 4

1 tablespoon vegetable oil
1 cup chopped onion
1 teaspoon grated ginger
$1/4$ teaspoon cayenne pepper
$1/2$ teaspoon turmeric
$1/2$ teaspoon cumin
4 chicken thighs
2 chicken breasts, cut in half
2 tablespoons toasted slivered almonds
1 cinnamon stick
1 teaspoon allspice
2 teaspoons orange peel, cut in thin slivers
1 teaspoon sugar
2 cups chicken stock or reduced-sodium chicken broth
1 cup water
2 carrots, sliced diagonally into $1/4$-inch coins
$1/4$ cup currants
1 cup rice; use basmati rice, if available
$1 1/2$ pounds cauliflower, cut into 1-inch florets
1 cup frozen peas, defrosted

1. In a heavy, wide-bottomed saucepan, large skillet, or paella pan, heat oil over medium heat. Add onion and ginger and cook until onion is translucent. Add cayenne, turmeric, and cumin and cook one minute longer.

2. Add chicken pieces and brown lightly, about 5 minutes. Stir in almonds, cinnamon stick, allspice, orange peel, and sugar. Add stock and water, cover and simmer for 15 minutes. Add carrots and cook for another 15 minutes.

3. Stir currants and rice into pan. Cover and simmer on low heat until rice is tender, 30 to 35 minutes, stirring twice during cooking. Meanwhile, steam cauliflower florets to crisp-tender (instructions, p. 129). Add peas to steamer for 1 minute to heat through. Set aside.

4. When rice is cooked, remove pan from heat. Add steamed cauliflower and peas, stir gently and set aside, covered, for 10 minutes before serving.

CAULIFLOWER, POTATO, AND CHICK-PEA CURRY

This is a great homestyle Indian curry. Serve it with basmati rice for a hearty and healthful meal.

Preparation time: 5 minutes
Cooking time: 20 to 25 minutes
Serves 4

> 2 tablespoons vegetable oil
> 3 or 4 medium potatoes, peeled and cut into ¹/₂-inch cubes (3 ¹/₂ cups)
> 1 cup chopped onion
> 2 teaspoons grated ginger
> 4 teaspoons curry powder
> ¹/₂ teaspoon cinnamon
> ¹/₂ teaspoon cumin
> 1 head cauliflower, broken into bite-size florets
> 2 cups chicken stock or reduced-sodium chicken broth
> 1¹/₂ cups cooked or canned chick-peas; if canned, rinse and drain
> ¹/₂ teaspoon salt, or to taste
> 1 cup plain low-fat yogurt

1. Heat oil in a large, wide-bottomed pot over medium-high heat. Add potatoes and cook until golden on all sides. Remove potatoes from pan and set aside on paper towels.

2. Add onions to pot and cook until translucent. Add ginger and spices and continue cooking until fragrant,

about 30 seconds. Stir cauliflower and potatoes into spice mixture, add broth and bring to a boil.

3. Reduce heat and simmer for 10 minutes. Add chickpeas and salt, if desired, and continue cooking until vegetables are tender. Stir in yogurt, heat through and serve.

 **MOROCCAN ROOT VEGETABLE STEW**

No broccoli? Turnips are cruciferous, too! This delicious vegetable stew has the flavors of Morocco; ladle it into the center of a bowl of steaming couscous.

Preparation time: 15 minutes
Cooking time: 50 to 60 minutes
Serves 4 to 5

1 tablespoon vegetable oil
1 cup chopped onion
$^1/_2$ cup chopped celery
3 cloves garlic, minced
$1^1/_2$ teaspoons cumin
$^1/_2$ teaspoon freshly ground black pepper
1 cinnamon stick
1 bay leaf
4 medium turnips, peeled and cut into $^1/_2$- to $^3/_4$-inch cubes (3 cups)
2 small sweet potatoes, peeled and cut into $^1/_2$- to $^3/_4$-inch cubes (2 cups)
1 or 2 carrots, peeled and cut into $^1/_2$- to $^3/_4$-inch cubes ($1^1/_2$ cups)
1 small parsnip, peeled and cut into $^1/_2$- to $^3/_4$-inch cubes ($1^1/_2$ cups)
$^1/_4$ cup chopped parsley
1 cup canned plum tomatoes, drained (reserve juice)

1. Heat oil in a heavy, wide-bottomed pot, over medium heat. Add onions and celery and cook until translu-

cent. Add garlic and continue cooking for 1 minute. Add cumin and pepper and cook for another minute, stirring.

2. Stir remaining ingredients into pot. Add reserved tomato juice and enough water to make 3 cups of liquid. Simmer, partially covered until vegetables are tender, 45 to 55 minutes, removing cinnamon stick after 25 minutes. Serve.

Risotto Primavera

It is difficult to give an exact recipe for risotto because cooking time will vary with the type and age of the rice, the heat of the stove and temperature of the stock. If you run out of stock before the rice is tender, add water instead.

Preparation time: 8 minutes
Cooking time: 30 to 35 minutes
Serves 6

> 8 cups chicken stock or reduced-sodium chicken broth
> 1 tablespoon olive oil
> 1 carrot, cut into $^1/_4$-inch pieces ($^1/_2$ cup)
> $^1/_2$ cup chopped shallots
> 2 cups arborio or Italian medium-grain rice
> 1$^1/_2$ pounds broccoli, broken into $^1/_2$-inch florets, stems peeled and cut into $^1/_4$-inch pieces
> $^1/_4$ cup tomato, seeded and cut into $^1/_4$-inch pieces
> $^1/_4$ cup frozen peas, thawed
> 2 tablespoons lemon juice
> 2 tablespoons grated Parmesan cheese
> Salt and freshly ground pepper, to taste

1. In a saucepan, heat chicken broth to boiling. Lower heat to simmer.

2. Heat oil in a heavy, wide-bottomed, 4$^1/_2$-quart saucepan, over medium-low heat. Add carrots and shallots and cook until shallots are translucent, about 3 min-

utes. Add rice and cook, stirring constantly until rice is well coated, $1^{1}/_{2}$ to 2 minutes.

3. Barely cover rice with broth and continue cooking, stirring until broth is almost all absorbed. Continue adding broth, $^{1}/_{2}$ cup at a time, stirring and cooking until broth is absorbed and rice comes away from side of pot before each addition. Continue until almost all of broth has been absorbed, 15 to 20 minutes.

4. Add broccoli, tomatoes, peas, and lemon juice and continue cooking and adding stock, $^{1}/_{4}$ cup at a time, until rice is creamy yet firm in center. This should take another 5 to 10 minutes.

5. Remove from heat, stir in cheese, salt and pepper. Serve with extra Parmesan cheese on the side.

BROCCOLI OR KALE CHEESE QUICHE

This quiche can be made either with or without a crust. To make it crustless, simply grease the inside of the pie plate and bake as usual.

Preparation time: 10 minutes
Baking time: 35 to 40 minutes
Serves 6

1 pie crust
1 teaspoon olive or vegetable oil
$^1/_4$ cup chopped onion, or $^3/_4$ cup if using kale
$^1/_2$ pound broccoli, chopped into $^1/_2$-inch pieces
   (2 cups) or 2 cups chopped kale
$^1/_2$ cup diced red pepper
2 tablespoons water
$^1/_2$ teaspoon freshly ground black pepper
$^1/_2$ teaspoon salt
$^3/_4$ cup grated reduced-fat cheddar cheese
1 cup egg substitute
$^1/_2$ cup skim milk
1 teaspoon mustard
$^1/_4$ teaspoon nutmeg
2 tablespoons grated Parmesan cheese

1. Preheat oven to 350°F. Prick bottom and sides of pie crust and bake until it just begins to color, about 10 minutes.

2. In a nonstick skillet, heat oil and cook onions, over medium heat, for 1 minute. Add broccoli and red pep-

per and continue cooking, stirring until well combined. Add water, cover and cook until vegetables are
crisp-tender, 2 to 3 minutes. Pepper and salt to taste.

3. Place cooked vegetables in pie crust and cover with
   cheddar cheese. Mix together egg substitute, milk,
   mustard, and nutmeg and pour over vegetables and
   cheese. Sprinkle with Parmesan cheese.

4. Bake until top is golden and puffed and quiche is set,
   35 to 40 minutes. Allow to cool slightly (5 to 10 mins.)
   before cutting.

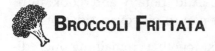
BROCCOLI FRITTATA

I have always found frittatas to be the best use for leftover potatoes. Add broccoli, reduce the fat with an egg substitute, and enjoy a healthful version of this classic.

Preparation time: 10 minutes
Cooking time: 15 minutes
Serves 4

2 teaspoons olive oil
$^1/_2$ cup chopped onions
1 medium potato, peeled, cooked, and sliced $^1/_8$-inch thick and cut into 1-inch pieces (1 cup)
2 cups $^1/_2$-inch broccoli florets, steamed to crisp-tender (instructions, see p. 129)
1 cup chopped broccoli florets
$^1/_4$ cup chives or scallions (green part only), thinly sliced
$^1/_4$ cup diced red bell pepper
1 cup cherry tomatoes, seeded and slivered
1 tablespoon chopped parsley
$^1/_2$ cup diced part-skim or nonfat mozzarella
$^1/_4$ cup slivered ham (optional)
1 tablespoon tomato paste
$1^1/_4$ cups fat-free egg substitute
$^1/_2$ teaspoon freshly ground black pepper, or to taste
$^1/_2$ teaspoon salt, or to taste

1. Preheat broiler. While broiler is heating, cook onions with oil, in a 10-inch nonstick skillet, over medium

heat, until translucent. Add potato and cook until browned. Be sure to tilt pan so oil covers sides of pan.

2. In a separate bowl mix together remaining ingredients.

3. Add mixture to hot skillet and flatten with a spatula. Cook until egg is almost set, lifting sides of fritatta to allow raw egg to run underneath.

4. Place skillet under broiler to finish cooking, 4 to 5 minutes. Be sure to keep handle of skillet out of oven to avoid melting it or burning yourself. Slide frittata onto a plate, cut into wedges and serve.

BAKED POTATO WITH BROCCOLI AND CHEESE

This is a great double-baked potato! Light and fresh tasting—it makes a great meal.

Preparation time: 5 minutes, plus baking time for potatoes
Cooking time: 20 to 30 minutes
Serves 4

2 Idaho potatoes, baked
2 cups chopped broccoli, steamed to crisp-tender
    (instructions, see p. 129)
$^1/_4$ cup cottage cheese
$^1/_4$ cup part-skim or nonfat ricotta
2 tablespoons shredded reduced-fat cheddar cheese
1 medium tomato, chopped ($^1/_2$ cup)
$^1/_4$ cup chives or scallions, green part only, thinly
    sliced
1 teaspoon chopped fresh or $^1/_2$ teaspoon dried
    rosemary
1 clove garlic, minced
1 teaspoon white wine vinegar
$^1/_4$ teaspoon salt
$^1/_2$ teaspoon freshly ground black pepper

(Continued on next page)

1. Preheat oven to 375°F.

2. Cut potatoes in half and scoop potato from skin. Reserve shells and combine potato with remaining ingredients.

3. Refill shells with potato mixture and form a mound on top. Place potatoes in oven and bake until hot, 20 to 30 minutes. Serve hot.

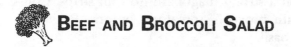

BEEF AND BROCCOLI SALAD

This salad can also be made with leftover steak. It has a lovely Italian flavor and is a great way to help meat eaters enjoy their vegetables.

Preparation time: 5 minutes, plus 15 minutes to marinate
Cooking time: 5 minutes
Serves 4

$^3/_4$ **pound flank steak**
2 tablespoons, plus 2 teaspoons soy sauce
1 tablespoon vegetable oil
1$^1/_4$ pounds broccoli, broken into 1-inch florets,
stems peeled and cut into $^1/_4$-inch diagonal slices,
steamed to crisp-tender (instructions, see p. 129)
2 medium tomatoes, diced (1 cup)
$^1/_2$ cup diced onion
2 tablespoons grated Parmesan cheese
2 tablespoons chopped fresh basil
2 tablespoons balsamic vinegar
1 teaspoon freshly ground black pepper
Arugula and radicchio leaves

1. Slash each side of steak 3 times with a sharp knife and cut it into 3 or 4 long strips 1 to 1$^1/_2$ inches wide. Marinate beef in 2 tablespoons soy sauce for 15 minutes. Heat 1 teaspoon of oil in a nonstick skillet, over high heat. Sear meat on all sides until cooked to medium rare. Allow steak to rest until cool before slicing.

2. Slice steak on a strong diagonal into thin strips. Combine beef with broccoli, tomatoes, onions, Parmesan cheese, and basil.

3. Stir together remaining oil, remaining soy sauce, balsamic vinegar, and pepper. Toss with beef mixture and serve on a bed of arugula and radicchio.

ORIENTAL BROCCOLI AND CHICKEN SALAD

This is a lovely salad with an Asian accent. The chicken can be baked, boiled, or bought precooked. It can also be an exciting use for leftover chicken.

Preparation time: 12 to 15 minutes
Cooking time: None
Serves 4

> 12 ounces cooked chicken, fat and skin removed, torn into pieces
> 3 cups broccoli florets (1 bunch), broken into 1-inch pieces, steamed to crisp-tender (instructions, see p. 129)
> 2 carrots, cut in thin diagonal slices (1 cup)
> 5 scallions, cut in long diagonal slivers ($^1/_2$ cup)
> $^1/_2$ red bell pepper, cut in thin slivers ($^1/_2$ cup)
> 1 clove garlic, minced
> 1 teaspoon grated ginger
> 1 tablespoon lemon juice
> 1 tablespoon orange juice
> $^1/_2$ teaspoon soy sauce
> $^1/_2$ teaspoon Oriental sesame oil
> 1 tablespoon vegetable oil
> $^1/_8$ teaspoon Oriental hot pepper oil, if available

1. Place chicken, broccoli, carrots, scallions, and red pepper in a large bowl.

2. Mix together remaining ingredients and pour over chicken and vegetables. Toss gently and serve.

SHRIMP, BROCCOLI, AND RICE SALAD WITH FRESH HERBS

This is a very fresh salad which is perfect in the summertime when fresh herbs are available. It is especially delicious if it has time to marinate before serving.

Preparation time: 5 minutes
Cooking time: None
Serves 4

1 pound large cooked shrimp, peeled and deveined
4 cups broccoli (1 large bunch), broken into $1/2$-inch florets, steamed to crisp-tender (instructions, see p. 129)
$1/2$ cup diced plum tomatoes
2 cups cooked brown rice
2 teaspoons olive oil
2 teaspoons lemon juice
1 teaspoon mustard
1 clove garlic, minced
$1/4$ teaspoon freshly ground black pepper
$1/4$ teaspoon salt, or to taste
2 teaspoons lemon peel, cut in thin slivers
2 tablespoons chopped fresh tarragon
2 tablespoons chopped fresh chives
2 tablespoons chopped fresh dill
12 crisp lettuce leaves, preferably radicchio or romaine

1. Combine first four ingredients in a nonmetal bowl. Stir together remaining ingredients except lettuce, also in a nonmetal bowl.

2. Pour dressing over rice mixture and toss. Serve on lettuce leaves.

FRUITED TUNA AND BROCCOLI SALAD

Use low-salt, water-packed tuna if you can find it. Or even better—use freshly cooked tuna!

Preparation time: 10 minutes
Cooking time: None
Serves 6

> **2 6 ¹/₈-ounce cans water-packed tuna, drained**
> **2 cups chopped broccoli stems (1 bunch)**
> **¹/₄ cup chopped Granny Smith apple**
> **1 cup halved red seedless grapes**
> **¹/₄ cup diced red onion**
> **2 tablespoons reduced-calorie mayonnaise**
> **¹/₃ cup plain low-fat yogurt**
> **1 teaspoon grated lemon zest**
> **1 teaspoon red wine vinegar**
> **1 teaspoon freshly ground black pepper, or to taste**
> **1 cup broccoli florets, broken into ¹/₂-inch pieces, steamed to crisp-tender (instructions, see p. 129)**

1. In a large bowl, break up tuna and combine with broccoli stems, apple, ³/₄ of the grapes, and onion.

2. In a separate bowl, mix together mayonnaise, yogurt, lemon zest, vinegar, and pepper. Stir into tuna mixture. Serve topped with reserved grape halves and broccoli florets.

Pastas, Pizzas, and Breads

ITALIAN-STYLE PASTA WITH BROCCOLI BUDS

Here is a version of a classic Italian pasta dish. The flavors are very fresh and the colors are bright and beautiful.

Preparation time: 10 minutes
Cooking time: Depends upon type of pasta used
Serves 4 to 5

- 1 pound pasta (ziti, penne, or fusilli)
- 2 tablespoons olive oil
- 4 cloves garlic, minced
- 1 cup finely chopped onion
- 6 cups broccoli florets (2 bunches), broken into bite-size pieces, steamed to crisp-tender (instructions, see p. 129)
- 2 cups canned plum tomatoes, seeded and diced (reserve liquid)
- 18 black olives, pitted and sliced
- 2 tablespoons capers, drained
- 1 tablespoon lemon juice
- Freshly ground black pepper
- 4 tablespoons thinly shredded fresh basil
- Parmesan cheese

1. In a large pot, cook pasta according to package directions.

2. Heat oil in a large nonstick skillet over medium heat. Add garlic and cook, stirring until soft, about 1 minute. Add onion and cook until translucent, 3 to 5 minutes.

3. Add broccoli, tomatoes, olives, capers, lemon juice, and $1/2$ cup liquid from tomatoes. Continue cooking, stirring occasionally until broccoli is tender, about 5 minutes. Add cooked pasta, pepper, and basil. Toss and serve with grated Parmesan cheese.

PASTA WITH CLAM SAUCE AND BROCCOLI

The Italians discovered a long time ago that broccoli works beautifully with shellfish. Here is a fresh white clam sauce mixed with broccoli. *Buono appetito!*

Preparation time: 10 minutes
Cooking time: 15 minutes
Serves 4

> 1 pound linguini
> 2 dozen clams, washed well
> $^1/_2$ cup water
> 1 tablespoon olive oil
> $^1/_2$ cup chopped onions
> $^1/_3$ cup white wine
> 1 tablespoon dried basil
> 1$^1/_2$ pounds broccoli, florets broken into $^1/_2$-inch
>   pieces, stems peeled and chopped
> Salt to taste
> Freshly ground black pepper to taste

1. In a large pot, cook linguini according to package directions.

2. Place clams and water in a large pot over high heat. Steam until clams open, 3 to 5 minutes. Remove from heat, pour liquid into a bowl. Discard any unopened shells and sand. Take clams from shells and place in liquid.

3. Heat oil in a nonstick skillet, over medium heat. Add onions and cook until translucent. Add clam liquid, minus clams and about 1 tablespoon liquid (to keep them moist), wine, basil, and broccoli. Cover and cook until broccoli is tender, 4 to 5 minutes. Meanwhile, chop clams.

4. Empty cooked linguini into skillet, toss with sauce and reserved clams and season with salt and pepper. Serve.

PENNE WITH SCALLOPS, SHRIMP, AND BROCCOLI

This is one of my favorite recipes. Try to use fresh tarragon and a good brand of crushed tomatoes; the ones imported from Italy are the best.

Preparation time: 10 minutes
Cooking time: 18 to 20 minutes
Serves 5 to 6

$^3/_4$ **pound penne or ziti cut pasta**
6 cups broccoli florets, cut in 1-inch pieces
1 tablespoon olive oil
$^1/_2$ **cup chopped onion**
3 tablespoons chopped shallots
$^1/_2$ **pound bay scallops or sea scallops cut into**
    $^1/_2$**-inch slices**
$^3/_4$ **cup crushed tomatoes**
$^1/_2$ **cup white wine**
1 red bell pepper, cut in $^1/_4$**-inch by** $1^1/_2$**-inch sticks**
    (1 cup)
1 tablespoon chopped fresh tarragon, or $1^1/_2$
    teaspoons dried tarragon
$^1/_4$ **teaspoon red pepper flakes**
Salt to taste
Freshly ground black pepper to taste
$^1/_3$ **cup plain low-fat or nonfat yogurt**
$^1/_2$ **pound large shrimp, peeled and deveined, cut**
    into $^1/_2$**-inch pieces**
3 tablespoons chopped parsley

1. In a large pot, cook pasta according to package directions. Add broccoli to cooking water for last 3 minutes of cooking. Drain.

2. In a large nonstick skillet, heat olive oil over medium heat. Add onions and shallots and cook, stirring constantly until onions are translucent, about 3 minutes. Add scallops and cook, stirring frequently until opaque, 3 to 4 minutes. Remove scallops from pan. Set aside.

3. Add tomatoes, wine, bell pepper, tarragon, red pepper flakes, salt, and black pepper to skillet. Cook for 2 minutes, stirring frequently until sauce has thickened slightly. Add shrimp, and yogurt, stir and cook until shrimp are pink, about 1 minute. Return scallops to pan, add pasta and broccoli and heat through. Serve promptly.

CHICKEN, BROCCOLI, AND MUSHROOM FETTUCINI

This dish makes an elegant pasta dinner. Serve it with a glass of white wine and a mixed green salad.

Preparation time: 10 minutes
Cooking time: 20 minutes
Serves 4 to 5

1 pound fettucini
4 cups broccoli florets, cut in $^1/_2$-inch pieces (1 large bunch)
2 tablespoons olive oil
1 pound skinned and boned chicken breast, sliced into long strips
3 cloves garlic, minced
$^1/_3$ pound leeks, washed, split lengthwise and cut in $^1/_2$-inch slices (2 cups)
3 cups sliced mushrooms
$^1/_2$ cup white wine
$^1/_4$ cup chicken stock or reduced-sodium broth
1 teaspoon fresh or $^1/_2$ teaspoon dried sage
$^1/_4$ teaspoon salt
$^1/_3$ cup low-fat milk
1 tablespoon flour
2 tablespoons grated Parmesan cheese

1. In a large pot, cook fettucini according to package directions. Add broccoli to cooking water for last 3 minutes of cooking. Drain well.

2. Heat oil in a large nonstick skillet over medium heat. Add chicken pieces and cook, stirring, until golden and cooked through, 3 to 4 minutes. Remove chicken from skillet and set aside. Add garlic to skillet and cook for 1 minute. Add leeks and cook, stirring frequently until wilted, 2 to 3 minutes. Add mushrooms and cook until golden.

3. Add wine, broth, sage and salt to skillet. Stir and heat to boiling. Stir together milk and flour until there are no lumps. Add milk and flour mixture gradually to skillet, stirring constantly. Continue stirring until thick.

4. Add pasta, broccoli, and chicken to skillet and toss with sauce and Parmesan cheese. Serve promptly.

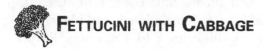

FETTUCINI WITH CABBAGE

The slight bitterness of sautéed cabbage works beautifully with pasta. Here the cabbage and onion are shredded to complement the length of the linguini.

Preparation time: 5 minutes
Cooking time: 10 minutes
Serves 4 to 5

  1 pound linguini
  1 tablespoon olive oil
  2 cloves garlic, minced
  2 medium onions, sliced thinly in circles and cut into
    semicircles
  2 pounds green cabbage, sliced thinly and separated
    into shreds
  2 red bell peppers, cut in long, thin strips (2 cups)
  12 black olives, pitted and sliced lengthwise into
    strips
  1 cup chicken stock or reduced-sodium chicken broth
  2 teaspoons lemon juice
  1/4 teaspoon freshly ground black pepper

1. In a large pot, cook pasta according to package directions.

2. Meanwhile, heat olive oil in a large nonstick skillet, over medium heat. Add garlic and cook until it begins to color. Add onions and cabbage and cook, stirring occasionally until wilted and beginning to brown, about 5 minutes.

3. Add red pepper and olives, and cook 1 minute. Increase heat and add stock, lemon juice, and black pepper. Cook until stock thickens, 2 to 4 minutes. Empty cooked and drained linguini into skillet. Toss and serve.

ANGEL HAIR PRIMAVERA WITH CREAMY TOMATO SAUCE

The pasta that you want to buy for this dish is capellini, the thinnest long pasta available from Italian dried pasta manufacturers. If you cannot find it, use thin spaghetti. Cauliflower plus broccoli make this dish very healthful.

Preparation time: 15 minutes
Cooking time: 30 to 35 minutes
Serves 5 to 6

5 teaspoons olive oil
$^1/_2$ cup chopped onion
4 cloves garlic, minced
$^1/_4$ cup chopped carrot
1 28-ounce can Italian peeled plum tomatoes
$^1/_4$ teaspoon dried thyme
1 bay leaf
$^1/_4$ teaspoon salt, or to taste
$^1/_4$ teaspoon pepper, or to taste
2 $^1/_2$ cups cauliflower florets ($^1/_2$ head), cut into
   $^1/_2$-inch pieces steamed to crisp-tender
1$^1/_2$ cups broccoli florets ($^1/_2$ bunch), broken into
   $^1/_2$-inch pieces, steamed to crisp-tender
1 small yellow squash, cut into $^1/_2$-inch cubes, lightly
   steamed (1 cup)
$^1/_2$ zucchini, cut into $^1/_2$-inch cubes, lightly steamed
   (1 cup)
$^1/_2$ cup frozen peas, defrosted
1 pound capellini

1 cup evaporated skim milk
¹/₄ cup grated Parmesan cheese

1. In a large nonstick skillet, heat 1 tablespoon oil over medium heat. Add onion and cook, stirring until translucent. Add 1 tablespoon of garlic and the chopped carrot and cook until garlic is soft. Stir in tomatoes, thyme, bay leaf, salt and pepper. Lower heat and gently simmer, stirring occasionally, until thick, 20 to 25 minutes. Cool slightly.

2. Meanwhile, in another large nonstick skillet, heat remaining oil, over medium heat. Add remaining garlic and cook until soft. Add vegetables and cook, stirring, until golden, 3 to 4 minutes. Set aside.

3. In a large pot, cook pasta according to package directions. Remove bay leaf from sauce. Pour tomato sauce into bowl of food processor. Process until smooth. With a rubber spatula, push sauce through a sieve, back into skillet, to remove seeds. Add milk and cheese and heat, over a low flame, until cheese is melted and incorporated.

4. Toss cooked pasta with sauce and vegetables. Serve in shallow bowls with grated Parmesan on side.

For crisp-tender steaming of vegetables, see page 129.

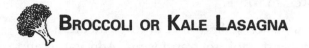 BROCCOLI OR KALE LASAGNA

Making lasagna is a time-consuming task—but well worth it. Try making two and freezing one!

Preparation time: 20 to 25 minutes
Baking time: 45 to 55 minutes
Serves 6

    2 tablespoons olive oil
    2 cups chopped onion
    5 cloves garlic, minced
    10 ounces mushrooms, finely chopped
    1 cup grated carrot
    1 1/2 pounds broccoli, florets chopped and stems
       peeled and chopped (5 cups) or 1 bunch kale,
       chopped
    1/4 teaspoon dried thyme
    1/4 teaspoon dried oregano
    1 1/4 cups reduced-fat ricotta cheese
    1 cup low-fat cottage cheese
    1/3 cup nonfat egg substitute
    1/2 teaspoon freshly ground black pepper
    1/4 cup chopped fresh basil
    2 tablespoons grated Parmesan cheese
    3 1/2 cups tomato sauce
    1/2 pound lasagna noodles, boiled to just tender
    1 cup shredded part-skim or nonfat mozzarella

(*Continued on next page*)

1. Preheat oven to 375°F.

2. In a large nonstick skillet, heat oil over medium heat. Add onions and cook to translucent. Add garlic and cook until golden. Add mushrooms and cook until dry, 4 to 5 minutes. Add carrot, broccoli or kale, thyme, and oregano, stir to combine, cover and cook until broccoli or kale is tender. Remove lid to allow any extra liquid to evaporate.

3. Combine ricotta, cottage cheese, egg substitute, pepper, basil, and Parmesan cheese.

4. In a 13-inch by 9-inch baking dish, spread $1/2$ cup of tomato sauce. Then lay down a layer of lasagna noodles, a layer of ricotta mixture, a layer of broccoli mixture, and 1 cup tomato sauce. Repeat. Top with another layer of noodles and remaining tomato sauce.

5. Sprinkle with mozzarella and bake until lasagna is bubbling and cheese is melted, 30 to 35 minutes. Let stand for 10 minutes before cutting.

 ## BROCCOLI PESTO PASTA

Some of the best dishes are the simplest. This one is so fresh and easy to make and the recipe can be doubled, tripled, quadrupled . . . enjoy!

Preparation time: 5 minutes
Cooking time: Pasta cooking time
Serves 4 (Yield: 1 cup pesto sauce)

  2 cups fresh basil leaves, rinsed well and dried
    thoroughly
  $1/2$ cup flat leaf Italian parsley leaves, rinsed well and
    dried thoroughly
  $1/4$ cup low-fat or nonfat ricotta cheese
  3 cloves garlic, minced
  2 tablespoons pignoli nuts or chopped walnuts
  3 tablespoons grated Parmesan cheese
  $1/2$ teaspoon freshly ground black pepper
  2 tablespoons olive oil
  2 tablespoons water
  $1/4$ teaspoon salt, or to taste
  1 pound pasta, preferably a strong shape such as ziti,
    penne, or rigatoni
  3 cups broccoli florets

1. Place basil, parsley, ricotta, garlic, nuts, cheese, pepper, oil, water, and salt in bowl of food processor. Pulse processor until mixture becomes a smooth paste. Pulsing prevents ingredients from sticking to sides of bowl. If they do anyway, simply push them back down.

2. Meanwhile, in a large pot, cook pasta according to package directions. Add broccoli to cooking liquid for last 3 minutes of cooking. Strain pasta and broccoli together, reserving $1/4$ cup of liquid.

3. Toss together broccoli and pasta, basil mixture, and reserved water. Serve.

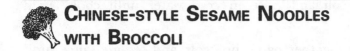 CHINESE-STYLE SESAME NOODLES WITH BROCCOLI

Here is a lighter version of the Chinese restaurant classic. It's also a sure way to get the children to eat their broccoli!

Preparation time: 5 minutes
Cooking time: Pasta cooking time
Serves 2 to 3

2 tablespoons soy sauce
2 tablespoons peanut butter
1 tablespoon Oriental sesame oil
1 tablespoon white vinegar
$^1/_4$ cup plain low-fat yogurt
1 teaspoon grated ginger
2 cloves garlic, minced
Hot pepper oil, to taste
$^1/_2$ pound linguini or Chinese noodles
1 pound broccoli, broken into 1-inch florets, stems peeled and cut into $^1/_4$-inch by 1-inch sticks
$^1/_4$ cup diced red bell pepper
1 teaspoon sesame seeds

1. In a bowl, whisk together first eight ingredients until well blended.

2. Meanwhile, in a large pot, cook pasta according to package directions. Add broccoli to cooking liquid for last 3 minutes of cooking. Drain pasta and

broccoli and rinse in cold water until cool. Drain well.

3. Toss together pasta, broccoli, and sesame sauce until well coated. Sprinkle with red peppers and sesame seeds and serve.

BROCCOLI RED PEPPER PIZZA

Once you know how to make pizza, there's no limit to the variations. Broccoli just happens to be a fabulous topping. You can make the dough ahead of time, defrost it in the refrigerator, and bring it to room temperature before shaping.

Preparation time: 20 minutes, plus rising time for dough,
* 5 minutes for topping*
Baking time: 15 to 20 minutes
Serves 4

Dough

  1 package dry yeast
  1 cup warm water
  2¹/₂ to 3 cups all-purpose flour
  1 tablespoon olive oil
  ¹/₂ teaspoon salt

Topping

  4 cups broccoli florets (1 large bunch), broken into
    ¹/₂-inch pieces, steamed to crisp-tender
    (instructions, see p. 129)
  10 olives, sliced
  3 roasted red peppers, cut into strips (instructions,
    see p. 74)
  ³/₄ cup tomato sauce
  ¹/₂ cup shredded part-skim or nonfat mozzarella

2 tablespoons grated Parmesan cheese
$^1/_2$ teaspoon oregano

1. Combine yeast, water, and 1 cup flour in a large bowl. Mix well and let stand for 5 minutes. Stir in $1^1/_2$ cups more flour, oil, and salt. With a spoon or your hands, mix dough until it holds its shape, adding more flour, if necessary.

2. Turn dough out onto a lightly floured surface and knead it until it is smooth and elastic. Add more flour, as necessary, if it becomes sticky.

3. Place dough in a large lightly oiled bowl, cover with towel or plastic wrap and allow it to rise until double in size, about 1 hour.

4. Preheat oven to 500°F. Divide dough into 4 equal-size balls, and allow them to rest for 15 minutes.

5. Press or roll each ball into a 6-inch round and place on a lightly oiled baking sheet. Crimp edges of each, sprinkle toppings evenly over surface, and place on bottom shelf of oven. Bake until edges are golden and cheese has melted, 15 to 20 minutes.

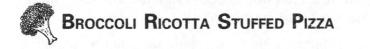

BROCCOLI RICOTTA STUFFED PIZZA

Here is a version of the classic stuffed pizza of Palermo, Italy. The recipe uses the same dough as the Broccoli Red Pepper Pizza, but is rolled somewhat thinner.

Preparation time: 15 minutes, plus dough preparation
Cooking time: 25 to 30 minutes
Makes 2 stuffed pizzas, 2 portions each

    1 tablespoon olive oil
    3 cloves garlic, chopped
    4 cups broccoli, steamed to crisp-tender
        (instructions, see p. 129) and chopped
    2 tablespoons chopped parsley
    1 cup part-skim or nonfat ricotta
    Salt to taste
    Freshly ground pepper to taste
    1/4 cup bread crumbs
    1 recipe for pizza dough (instructions, see p. 119–
        120)

1. Preheat oven to 450°F.

2. Heat olive oil in a nonstick skillet, over medium-low heat. Add garlic and cook until golden, 3 to 4 minutes. Add broccoli and cook, stirring frequently, for 3 minutes. Remove from heat, cool to room temperature and mix with parsley, ricotta, salt and pepper.

3. Roll dough into 4 11-inch rounds. Place 2 rounds on a lightly oiled baking sheet, sprinkle with 1/2 the bread

crumbs, spread with broccoli mixture and top with remaining bread crumbs.

4. Cover filling with two remaining rounds, pinching
   edges together to seal. Brush tops with water and place
   in oven to cook until golden, 25 to 30 minutes. Cool
   slightly before serving.

RED CABBAGE, CARAMELIZED ONIONS, AND GOAT CHEESE PIZZA

Follow the pizza dough instructions for Broccoli Red Pepper Pizza, but top it with this brilliant combination of flavors. The slow cooking of the onions brings out their natural sweetness—brilliantly contrasted with the bitterness of the cabbage.

Preparation time: 30 minutes, plus dough preparation
Baking time: 15 to 20 minutes
Serves 4

2 teaspoons olive oil
4 onions, thinly sliced
$1/2$ cup water
6 cups shredded red cabbage
$1/4$ cup vinegar
1 cup water
$1/2$ cup goat cheese, crumbled
Freshly ground black pepper to taste
Salt to taste
1 recipe for pizza dough (instructions, see p. 119–120)

1. Preheat the oven to 500°F.

2. Place olive oil, onion, and 2 tablespoons water in a medium skillet and cook, over low heat, until onions begin to brown, about 15 minutes. Add remaining water and continue cooking until onions are soft and sweet, another 15 to 20 minutes. Remove from heat.

3. In a saucepan, combine cabbage, vinegar, and 1 cup water. Cook, covered, over low heat until cabbage is tender, 10 to 15 minutes. Drain off excess water.

4. Roll out dough. Spread onion mixture evenly over surface of pizza dough rounds. Top with cabbage and sprinkle with goat cheese, pepper and salt.

5. Place on bottom shelf of oven and bake until edges are golden and cheese has melted, 15 to 20 minutes.

BROCCOLI CHEESE BREAD WITH THYME AND BASIL

This is a great sandwichlike treat. Try experimenting with different types of cheeses.

Preparation time: 10 minutes
Baking time: 20 to 25 minutes
Serves 4

    1 2-foot loaf French bread
    4 cups broccoli florets, broken into ¹/₂-inch pieces,
      steamed to crisp-tender (instructions, see p. 129)
    1 cup shredded part-skim or nonfat mozzarella
    ¹/₄ cup grated Parmesan cheese
    1 tablespoon fresh thyme leaves or 1 teaspoon dried
    3 tablespoons chopped fresh basil or 1 tablespoon
      dried basil
    3 cloves garlic, minced
    ¹/₄ teaspoon freshly ground black pepper
    ¹/₄ teaspoon salt

1. Preheat oven to 375°F. Slice bread lengthwise, but do not cut it all the way through. Set aside.

2. In a bowl, combine remaining ingredients and toss well. Without breaking bread apart, fill it with broccoli cheese mixture. Place stuffed bread in oven until cheese is melted and warm, 20 to 25 minutes. Slice and serve.

SIDE DISHES

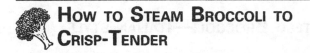

How to Steam Broccoli to Crisp-Tender

Steaming broccoli is one of the most healthful and beautiful ways to cook it. It becomes crisp-tender, free of the tough fiber of raw broccoli, yet crunchy and brilliant green.*

Preparation time: 2 minutes
Cooking time: 3 to 5 minutes
Serves 4 to 6

1 bunch broccoli, 1¹/₂ to 2 pounds

1. Rinse broccoli, remove florets from stalks. Separate florets into 1-inch clusters. Place in a steamer basket.

2. Cut ¹/₂ inch from tough end of broccoli stalk. With a vegetable peeler or sharp paring knife, peel off darker green outer skin. Cut into ¹/₄-inch diagonal slices, or another shape, as desired. Arrange on top of florets.

3. Place over gently boiling water and steam, covered, until crisp-tender, 3 to 5 minutes. Remove from steamer and serve with a sauce or rinse under cold water until cool, and set aside for future use.

---

* The same method may be used for cauliflower and brussels sprouts, but they will take a few minutes longer to cook.

SAUTÉED BROCCOLI—ITALIAN-STYLE

Here is a gorgeous garlicky Italian recipe! I use far less oil than the Italians and finish the cooking with water.

Preparation time: 5 minutes
Cooking time: 5 to 7 minutes
Serves 4

1 tablespoon olive oil
4 cloves garlic, minced
1¼ pounds broccoli, broken into 1-inch florets,
　　stems peeled and cut into ¼-inch diagonal slices
½ cup slivered red bell peppers
2 tablespoons chopped parsley
¼ teaspoon freshly ground black pepper
2 tablespoons water
1 tablespoon grated Parmesan cheese

1. In a large nonstick skillet, heat olive oil over medium heat, add garlic and cook, stirring constantly until garlic is just golden, about 2 minutes. Add broccoli and stems and cook for 1 minute.

2. Add red peppers, parsley, black pepper, and 2 tablespoons of water. Continue cooking until water is absorbed and broccoli is crisp-tender, 2 to 3 minutes.

3. Toss with Parmesan cheese and serve immediately.

ROASTED MIXED VEGETABLES

Roasting is one of the most delicious ways to prepare vegetables. This is a combination of my favorites, but you can experiment with fennel, zucchini, asparagus . . . use your imagination.

Preparation time: 10 minutes
Cooking time: 45 minutes
Serves 6

1 medium onion, cut in $^1/_2$-inch strips (1 cup)
1 yellow bell pepper, cut in $^1/_2$-inch strips (1 cup)
1 green bell pepper, cut in $^1/_2$-inch strips (1 cup)
3 plum tomatoes, cut in thin wedges
3 cloves garlic, sliced thinly
1 tablespoon fresh or $1^1/_2$ teaspoons dry thyme
$^1/_2$ teaspoon freshly ground black pepper
$1^1/_2$ tablespoons olive oil
2 cups broccoli florets, broken into 1-inch pieces ($^1/_2$ bunch)
2 cups cauliflower, cut in $^1/_2$-inch florets ($^1/_2$ head)
$1^1/_2$ teaspoons lemon juice
$^1/_2$ teaspoon salt, or to taste
1 tablespoon finely shredded fresh basil

1. Preheat oven to 400°F.

2. In one large or two small roasting pans combine onions, yellow and green peppers, tomatoes, garlic, $^1/_2$ of the thyme, $^1/_4$ teaspoon pepper, and 2 teaspoons of

olive oil. Place in oven and roast 25 minutes, tossing and mixing vegetables about halfway through.

3. Meanwhile, in a bowl combine broccoli, cauliflower, remaining thyme, pepper, and olive oil. When 25 minutes have passed, add broccoli and cauliflower mixture to roasting pans. Mix together and cook for 20 minutes more.

4. Remove vegetables from oven and toss with lemon juice, salt, and basil. Serve.

 **Vegetable Pâté**

This dish is ideal for a different type of side dish. It also looks very impressive when unmolded and sliced. Try to use kale rather than spinach—it's one of the less well-known cruciferous vegetables.

Preparation time: 25 minutes
Cooking time: 45 minutes
Serves 6 to 8

> 1 large or two small red peppers, roasted
> (instructions, see p. 74)
> 2 teaspoons cornstarch
> 4 teaspoons olive oil
> 1 cup finely chopped leek
> 2 cloves garlic, minced
> 5 ounces mushrooms, finely chopped
> 1 cup frozen chopped spinach, defrosted and well
> drained *or* 1 cup chopped kale, steamed until
> tender
> 3 cups finely chopped broccoli florets
> 1 cup finely chopped cauliflower
> 1 tablespoon lemon juice
> 1/2 teaspoon freshly ground black pepper
> Pinch nutmeg
> 1 teaspoon salt
> 1 cup reduced-fat ricotta
> 1 egg, lightly beaten
> 2 tablespoons finely chopped fresh basil

6 canned or frozen artichoke hearts, drained if
canned, defrosted if frozen, patted dry

1. Preheat oven to 350°F.

2. Toss red peppers with 2 teaspoons of oil and lay them
   along bottom of a lightly oiled loaf pan. Sprinkle peppers evenly with 1 teaspoon of cornstarch. Set aside.

3. In a large nonstick skillet, heat remaining oil over medium heat. Add leeks and cook until wilted. Add garlic
   and continue cooking for 1 minute. Add mushrooms,
   spinach, broccoli, cauliflower, lemon juice, pepper,
   nutmeg, and salt. Cook, stirring occasionally, until
   broccoli is tender and all the liquid has evaporated, 5
   or 6 minutes. Cool slightly.

4. Mix together ricotta, egg, basil, and remaining 1 teaspoon cornstarch and stir well. Combine ricotta and
   vegetable mixtures. Pour 1/2 of mixture into loaf pan,
   line artichoke hearts down center and top them with
   remaining broccoli mixture.

5. Bake in oven until firm, 45 minutes. Allow pâté to cool
   for at least 10 minutes, turn it out onto a plate and cut
   in 1-inch pieces. Serve hot or cold.

# SPICY BROCCOLI STIR-FRY

Crispy, fresh, and with just enough spice to keep your mouth tingling. Be sure that the chilies remain whole; if the seeds creep out, your mouth will be more than tingling!

Preparation time: 5 minutes
Cooking time: 5 minutes
Serves 4

1 tablespoon vegetable oil
4 cloves garlic, minced
2 teaspoons grated ginger
5 whole dried chili peppers
1 1/2 pounds broccoli, broken into 1-inch florets, stems peeled and cut into 1/4-inch diagonal slices, steamed to crisp-tender (instructions, see p. 129)
1 red bell pepper cut into 1/8 to 1/4-inch strips
2 teaspoons reduced-sodium soy sauce

1. Heat oil in a large nonstick skillet over medium-high heat. Add garlic, ginger, and chili peppers. Cook, stirring constantly, for 1 minute.

2. Add broccoli, red peppers, and soy sauce, and continue cooking and stirring until broccoli is well coated, about 3 minutes. Serve.

 CAULIFLOWER AU GRATIN

This is one dish where I like cauliflower very soft. If you prefer it crisper, don't steam it before baking. Try broccoli au gratin, too!

Preparation time: 10 minutes
Baking time: 40 minutes
Serves 4

1 head cauliflower, cut in 2-inch florets, steamed to crisp-tender (instructions, see p. 129)
2 tablespoons flour
2 cups low-fat milk
1 cup grated reduced-fat cheddar cheese
1 tablespoon grated Parmesan cheese
1 teaspoon mustard
Pinch nutmeg

1. Preheat oven to 375°F. Place cauliflower florets in a shallow baking dish. Set aside.

2. Combine flour and milk in a saucepan until smooth. Cook over medium-low heat, stirring, until it thickens, 4 to 5 minutes. Stir cheeses, mustard, and nutmeg into thickened milk until cheese is melted.

3. Pour cheese sauce over cauliflower. Place dish in oven and bake for 30 minutes. Serve hot.

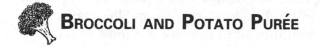 # BROCCOLI AND POTATO PURÉE

If you think purées are just for babies, you're missing out on a delightful dish. I serve this one with fish and a light tomato and herb sauce. Try it. . . .

Preparation time: 5 minutes
Cooking time: 20 minutes
Serves 4

>   2 medium-size potatoes, peeled and cut in 1¹/₂-inch
>   cubes
>   1 medium onion, cut in 1-inch pieces (¹/₂ cup)
>   2 cloves garlic
>   ¹/₂ pound broccoli, cut in 1-inch florets, stems peeled
>   and cut in 1-inch cubes
>   1¹/₂ teaspoons grated lemon zest
>   Freshly ground black pepper to taste
>   Salt to taste
>   ¹/₄ to ¹/₂ cup chicken stock or reduced-sodium
>   chicken broth as needed to make the mixture
>   almost smooth
>   2 tablespoons chopped parsley
>   1 tablespoon olive oil

1. Place potatoes, onion, and garlic in a medium-size saucepan. Add water to cover. Bring to a boil, reduce heat to medium and simmer, covered, for 14 minutes. Add broccoli and continue cooking until potatoes and broccoli are tender, about 6 minutes.

2. Combine broccoli-potato mixture, lemon zest, pepper and salt in bowl of food processor. Slowly add stock through feed tube until mixture is almost smooth.

3. Add parsley and continue to process, adding oil through feed tube in a thin stream. Process until smooth. Correct seasoning and serve.

 POTATO BROCCOLI CHEESE TERRINES

This is a variation of a recipe that I developed with Marie Simmons, an amazing food columnist and cookbook author who has shared with me a few of her jewels of culinary wisdom. It is so easy yet very impressive.

Preparation time: 5 minutes
Cooking time: 50 to 60 minutes
Serves 4

1 cup potatoes, peeled and very thinly sliced
1¹/₄ cups chopped broccoli florets
2 teaspoons fresh thyme leaves
¹/₄ cup goat cheese
¹/₂ teaspoon freshly ground pepper
¹/₂ teaspoon salt
2 teaspoons all-purpose flour
¹/₂ cup chicken stock or reduced-sodium chicken broth
¹/₄ cup low-fat milk

1. Preheat oven to 350°F.

2. Into 4 lightly oiled ¹/₂-cup soufflé or custard cups, sprinkle ¹/₃ of thyme and layer ¹/₃ of potatoes on top. Divide each of remaining ingredients in half. Layer the 4 cups evenly with ¹/₂ of goat cheese, ¹/₂ of broccoli, ¹/₂ of remaining thyme, ¹/₂ of flour, pepper, and salt. Cover with another layer of potatoes. Sprinkle again with remaining cheese, broccoli, thyme, flour, pepper, and salt. Top with remaining potatoes.

3. Pour 2 tablespoons of stock and 1 tablespoon milk over each terrine, cover with foil and place in oven on a baking sheet. Cook for 40 minutes, uncover, and continue cooking for 10 to 20 minutes until potatoes are soft.

4. Allow terrines to cool until liquid is absorbed, 10 to 15 minutes. Slide a knife around edge of each cup and turn terrines out onto a plate. Serve.

 # BROCCOLI CORN SOUFFLÉ

This is a variation of spoon bread, mixed with broccoli and corn. It's quite substantial and is delicious as a side dish for a midwinter meal or even as a meal on its own.

Preparation time: 15 minutes
Cooking time: 1 hour
Serves 4

  2 cups low-fat milk
  $^1/_2$ cup, plus 2 tablespoons, yellow cornmeal
  2 teaspoons vegetable oil
  1 cup chopped onion
  4 cups chopped broccoli (1 medium bunch), steamed to crisp-tender (instructions, see p. 129)
  $^1/_2$ teaspoon salt
  1 teaspoon freshly ground black pepper
  $^1/_2$ cup frozen corn kernels, defrosted
  1 teaspoon baking powder
  $^1/_2$ cup shredded low-fat or nonfat mozzarella
  2 tablespoons grated Parmesan cheese
  2 egg whites, beaten until stiff

1. Preheat oven to 375°F.

2. In a bowl, combine one cup of milk and cornmeal. In a large saucepan, heat remaining milk to just below boiling. Stir cornmeal mixture into hot milk. Cook over low heat, stirring frequently, until very thick, about 10 minutes. Cool slightly.

3. In a nonstick skillet, cook onions in oil, until translucent. Add broccoli and cook until well combined with onion. Season with salt and pepper and cool slightly.

4. To cornmeal mixture, add broccoli mixture, corn, baking powder, and cheeses. Stir well.

5. Beat egg whites until they form stiff peaks. Gently stir $1/2$ of egg whites into mixture, to lighten it. Carefully fold in remaining egg whites.

6. Place mixture in a greased casserole. Bake until golden, about 1 hour. Serve while hot.

BREADED BROCCOLI FLORETS

These oven-fried florets are crisp from their coating as well as from the broccoli. They are also delicious served with a dipping sauce such as honey-mustard or creamy horseradish and served as an appetizer.

Preparation time: 10 minutes
Cooking time: 10 minutes
Serves 4

2 egg whites, lightly beaten until foamy
1 teaspoon vegetable oil
1 tablespoon all-purpose flour
$^1/_2$ teaspoon salt
$^1/_2$ teaspoon freshly ground black pepper
1 teaspoon fresh or $^1/_2$ teaspoon dried thyme
2 cloves garlic, minced
1 teaspoon grated lemon zest
2 tablespoons grated Parmesan cheese
Pinch cayenne pepper
4 cups broccoli or cauliflower, cut in 1-inch pieces,
blanched in boiling water (1 minute for broccoli, 2
minutes for cauliflower)
1 cup bread crumbs

1. Preheat oven to 400°F.

2. Combine egg whites with oil and place in a shallow bowl. In a separate shallow bowl, combine remaining ingredients, except broccoli and bread crumbs.

3. Dip each floret into egg mixture and shake off excess. Roll in bread crumbs and place on a lightly oiled non-stick baking sheet. Repeat quickly with each floret.

4. Bake for 5 minutes, turn, and bake another 5 minutes.

Honey-Mustard Dipping Sauce

$1/4$ cup plain low-fat yogurt
4 teaspoons mustard
2 teaspoons honey

Stir all ingredients together until well blended.

# BROCCOLI "POTATO" PANCAKES

I found that these pancakes cook better in the oven than in a skillet, but feel free to make them stove-top. If you can afford the extra calories, they become crispy when cooked in oil.

Preparation time: 10 minutes
Cooking time: 15 to 18 minutes
Serves 4

$^1/_2$ cup grated onion
$^1/_4$ cup grated carrots
$1^1/_2$ cups peeled and grated broccoli stems
$^1/_2$ cup chopped broccoli buds
2 tablespoons chopped parsley
Salt and freshly ground pepper to taste
Pinch nutmeg
1 tablespoon all-purpose flour
2 tablespoons nonfat egg substitute
$^1/_4$ teaspoon baking soda

1. Preheat oven to 400°F.

2. Squeeze onions, carrots, and broccoli in cheesecloth or paper towels.

3. Combine grated vegetables, parsley, salt, pepper, and nutmeg in a large bowl. Add flour and toss gently to coat.

4. In a separate bowl, mix together egg substitute and baking soda. Pour over vegetable mixture.

5. Spray a nonstick baking sheet with cooking spray. Carefully place one tablespoonful of vegetable mixture at a time onto sheet and flatten. Cook until golden brown on one side, turn and cook until other side is brown, about 8 minutes per side.

5. Place in preheated 300°F. oven until all pancakes are made. Remove from oven and serve.

SHREDDED BRUSSELS SPROUTS WITH BACON

Brussels sprouts are fantastic shredded. They remain crisp and green and retain their pungent flavor.

Preparation time: 5 minutes
Cooking time: 8 minutes
Serves 4

10 ounces brussels sprouts, rinsed and ends trimmed
1 cup shredded carrots
2 tablespoons chopped raw bacon
$^1/_3$ cup chopped shallots
$^1/_2$ cup chicken stock or reduced-sodium chicken broth
$^1/_4$ teaspoon nutmeg
$^1/_4$ teaspoon freshly ground black pepper
$^1/_4$ teaspoon salt, or to taste
$^1/_4$ cup low-fat milk

1. Shred brussels sprouts in a food processor with regular blade, or chop well by hand. Combine with carrots.

2. Cook bacon in a large nonstick skillet over medium heat. Add shallots and cook until translucent. Add brussels sprouts and carrots, stirring until well coated.

3. Add stock, nutmeg, pepper, and salt. Stir and cover for 3 minutes or until brussels sprouts are crisp-tender. Add milk, stir, and continue cooking, uncovered, until liquid is absorbed. Serve.

GARLIC SAUTÉED KALE

I have always been a fan of spinach, but when I tasted kale I became a convert. This cruciferous vegetable retains its color and shape far better than the old standby. Sorry, Popeye!

Preparation time: 2 minutes
Cooking time: 6 to 8 minutes per batch
Serves 4

> **4 teaspoons olive oil**
> **6 cloves garlic, minced**
> **1 bunch kale, thick stems removed, cut in 1-inch**
>   **strips**
> **1 teaspoon salt**
> **¹/₃ cup water**

1. Prepare kale in two batches or two large nonstick skillets, dividing all ingredients in half.

2. Heat oil in large nonstick skillet(s) over medium heat. Add garlic and cook, stirring, until tender. Add kale and toss until evenly coated with oil. Add salt and water, cover, and cook until tender but still bright green, 5 to 7 minutes. Serve.

SAUTÉED CABBAGE DIJONNAISE

This dish is so simple, but so perfect tasting. Be sure to use a good dijon mustard because it will be the primary flavor.

Preparation time: 2 minutes
Cooking time: 4 to 5 minutes
Serves 4 to 5

   Vegetable oil for sautéing
   1 head green cabbage, cut into thin strips
   4 teaspoons olive oil
   1 tablespoon dijon mustard
   1 tablespoon red wine vinegar
   ¼ teaspoon freshly ground black pepper
   2 tablespoons chopped fresh basil

1. Heat oil in a nonstick skillet, over medium-high heat. Add cabbage and cook, stirring frequently, until cabbage is tender and beginning to brown.

2. Meanwhile, stir together the olive oil, mustard, vinegar, and pepper. When cabbage is done, toss with dressing and sprinkle with basil. Serve.

 ## LEMON-PEPPER SAUTÉED BROCCOLI

Broccoli and lemon are a classic combination. This is a delicious but simple sauté—fresh and crunchy!

Preparation time: 2 minutes
Cooking time: 6 minutes
Serves 4

> 1 tablespoon olive oil
> 1 1/4 pounds broccoli, broken into 1 1/2-inch florets, stems peeled and cut in 1/4-inch diagonal slices
> 1/2 lemon, sliced and seeded
> 2 teaspoons freshly ground black pepper
> 2 teaspoons lemon juice
> 1/3 cup water
> 1/2 teaspoon salt

1. Heat oil in a large nonstick skillet, over medium heat. Add broccoli, lemon slices, and pepper. Cook, stirring, until broccoli begins to brown slightly.

2. Add lemon juice, water, and salt. Cover and cook until broccoli is crisp-tender. Serve.

WILD RICE MUSHROOM
BROCCOLI SAUTÉ

This is a hearty dish which goes well with grilled meat. Try experimenting with different varieties of wild mushrooms for a different treat.

Preparation time: 5 minutes, plus 45 minutes to cook rice
Cooking time: 12 to 14 minutes
Serves 6

   1 tablespoon olive oil
   $^1/_2$ cup chopped shallots
   10 ounces mushrooms, cut in lengthwise wedges
   4 cups broccoli florets, broken into $^1/_2$-inch pieces (1
      large bunch)
   $^1/_2$ cup diced red bell pepper
   $^3/_4$ cup sherry
   $1^1/_2$ teaspoons fresh, or $^3/_4$ teaspoon dried rosemary
   1 cup wild rice, cooked (about 3 cups)

1. In a large nonstick skillet, cook olive oil and shallots over medium heat until translucent. Increase heat, add mushrooms, and cook until golden.

2. Add broccoli and red peppers, cover, and cook until broccoli is bright green, about 2 minutes.

3. Uncover, add sherry and rosemary, and cook, stirring, until sherry has reduced by $^1/_2$, 3 or 4 minutes.

4. Add cooked rice to pan, toss and serve.

BRAISED BROCCOLI AND ONION WITH RED WINE AND HERBS

Here is my version of a classic Italian preparation for broccoli. The broccoli does not retain its bright green color, but the flavor is excellent.

Preparation time: 10 minutes
Cooking time: 40 minutes
Serves 6

> 1³/₄-2 pounds broccoli, cut in 1-inch florets, stalks
>   peeled and cut into ¹/₄-inch diagonal slices
>   (6 cups)
> 4 medium onions, thinly sliced
> 1 cup seeded and slivered plum tomatoes
> 6 cloves garlic, thinly sliced
> 3 teaspoons fresh or 1¹/₂ teaspoons dried thyme
> 1 teaspoon dried oregano
> ¹/₂ teaspoon freshly ground black pepper
> ¹/₄ teaspoon salt or to taste
> 1 tablespoon olive oil
> ¹/₂ cup good quality red wine
> 2 tablespoons chopped fresh basil

1. Preheat oven to 375°F.

2. In a large bowl, toss together all ingredients, except wine and basil. Place mixture in a medium-size, non-metal baking dish.

3. Pour wine over mixture. Cover with aluminum foil and bake until vegetables are tender, about 40 minutes, uncovering dish after 30 minutes.

4. Top with chopped basil and serve promptly.

SWEET AND SOUR RED CABBAGE

This is, without a doubt, the best way to eat red cabbage. It is sweet, crunchy, and a brilliant shade of fuchsia.

Preparation time: 2 minutes
Cooking time: 30 to 40 minutes
Serves 4

- 1 tablespoon vegetable oil
- 3 tablespoons red wine vinegar
- 2 tablespoons honey
- 2 tablespoons water
- 1 teaspoon soy sauce
- 2 teaspoons sugar
- 1 2-pound head red cabbage, shredded

1. In a large saucepan, combine oil, vinegar, honey, water, soy sauce, and sugar. Heat over low heat until honey and sugar are dissolved. Increase heat and bring mixture to a boil.

2. Add cabbage and stir. Cover, lower heat, and simmer, stirring occasionally, until cabbage is tender, 30 to 40 minutes. Serve.

INDEX

ABOUT THE AUTHORS

Tamara Holt

An innovative caterer and professional recipe developer, Tamara Holt has a special flair for making healthful foods elegant and easy. Her training includes apprentice work at the New School Culinary Arts Program and recipe development and testing for several well-known cookbook authors. Tamara Holt is also the author of *Bean Power* in this series. She lives and works in New York City.

Marilynn Larkin

Marilynn Larkin is an award-winning medical journalist whose articles have appeared in a wide range of national consumer magazines and medical trade publications. She is a contributing editor for *Nutrition Forum* and a former contributing editor for *Health* magazine. She is also the author of two books to be published in the Dell Medical Library, *What You Can Do About Anemia* and *Relief from Chronic Sinusitis*. Marilynn Larkin lives and works in New York City.

FIX THEM PLAIN OR FANCY,
BEANS ARE THE FLAVORFUL WAY
TO PUT HEALTH ON YOUR TABLE
. . . FOR PENNIES!

South-of-the-Border Black Bean Dip
For parties or snacks, this tangy dip goes great with fresh salsa and salt-free tortilla or veggie chips . . . and you can mix it up in just three minutes.

Kidney Bean, Chicken, and Mango Salad
A delicious eight-minute marvel, this perfect summer meal looks beautiful on a bed of shredded romaine lettuce and tastes superb . . . a magnificent mix of flavors!

Split Pea and Spinach Soup
Sure to become a favorite for winter lunches, this satisfying "second-helping-good" soup is a nutrient-rich crowd pleaser.

Mexican Lasagne
A low-cost meal that can serve six, this unconventional, meatless version of lasagne will bring you bravos . . . and no one will guess that it's exceptionally high in fiber and nearly fat-free.

Lentil and Orange Salad
The brilliant contrast of the slightly nutty lentils with the sweet-and-sour orange makes this fast-to-fix lunch or first course an exotic treat.

Light-style Baked Beans with Ham
A lovely version of classic baked beans, it's redolent with the smoky flavor of ham and the subtle sweetness of spices and molasses.

CONTEMPORARY RECIPES FOR ALL TYPES OF
DRIED BEANS AND LEGUMES . . .
SPLIT PEAS, BLACK-EYED PEAS, LENTILS,
CHICK-PEAS, WHITE, NAVY, PINTO, KIDNEY, BLACK,
LIMA, AND SOYBEANS

BEAN
POWER

TAMARA HOLT

INTRODUCTION BY
MARILYNN LARKIN

A LYNN SONBERG BOOK

Published by
Dell Publishing
a division of
Bantam Doubleday Dell Publishing Group, Inc.
1540 Broadway
New York, New York 10036

If you purchased this book without a cover you should be aware that this book is stolen property. It was reported as "unsold and destroyed" to the publisher and neither the author nor the publisher has received any payment for this "stripped book."

Research about legumes and human health and nutrition is ongoing and subject to interpretation. Although every effort has been made to include the most up-to-date and accurate information in this book, there can be no guarantee that what we know about this subject won't change with time. The reader should bear in mind that this book should not be used for self-diagnosis or self-treatment and should consult appropriate medical professionals regarding all health issues and before making any major dietary changes.

Copyright © 1993 by Lynn Sonberg Book Services

All rights reserved. No part of this book may be reproduced or transmitted in any form or by any means, electronic or mechanical, including photocopying, recording, or by any information storage and retrieval system, without the written permission of the Publisher, except where permitted by law.

The trademark Dell® is registered in the U.S. Patent and Trademark Office.

ISBN: 0-440-21538-2

Published by arrangment with Lynn Sonberg Book Services, 166 East 56 Street, 3-C, New York, NY 10022

Printed in the United States of America

Published simultaneously in Canada

Bean Power is gratefully dedicated to my friends and family for their support, advice, and ideas through the development of this book. A special thank you to my mother, Shawn, and Wally for tasting the recipes and giving praise when it was most needed, and Rhea, Suzanna, Michael, and Gordon for listening to me when I was full of beans.

CONTENTS

MAIN DISHES

MAIN DISH SALADS

PASTAS

SALADS

SIDE DISHES

SWEETS

INTRODUCTION

Want to cut your risk of developing cancer? Combat heart disease? Keep your weight under control? Trim your food budget? One important step can set you on the path to all these goals: adding beans to your daily diet.

The American Cancer Society, the National Cancer Institute, the American Heart Association, and other leading health organizations are urging Americans to cut down on total fat intake and eat more high-fiber foods—easy to do when beans are on the menu! The reasons for these recommendations are twofold:

- A high-fat diet appears to play a role in the development of breast, colon, and prostate cancers. Too much dietary fat has also been implicated in heart disease. Of course, a high-fat diet can also make you fat—and obesity itself is a risk factor for a host of ills, including most major cancers, heart disease, high blood pressure, and adult-onset diabetes.

- A high-fiber diet, on the other hand, appears to protect against disease—reducing the risk of cancer, helping prevent heart disease, facilitating weight loss, and maintaining a desirable weight.

Amazingly, including beans at mealtime can help you follow *both* of these important health guidelines. Beans help you reduce the amount of fat in your diet primarily by acting as an alternative source of protein; instead of getting your protein from meat and poultry, which often contain high amounts of saturated animal fat, you can get this important nutrient from beans—which contain only very small amounts (in most cases less than one gram) of vegetable fat.

As far as fiber is concerned, beans in all their forms are *loaded* with this health-promoting nutrient: one cup of cooked kidney beans, for example, contains a whopping *12.2* grams of fiber, while one cup of cooked split peas— also part of the bean family—contains an incredible *16.2* grams of fiber, according to 1992 unpublished data from the U.S. Department of Agriculture, Human Nutrition Information Service. Nutrition experts advise eating between 20 and 30 grams of fiber daily to enjoy protective benefits—which means just a single serving of beans can meet *more than half* of our daily requirement.

In addition to protein and fiber, beans also contain generous amounts of other nutrients vital to good health: carbohydrates, the body's main fuel; B-vitamins, which play a key role in facilitating cell production and the maintenance of skin, eyes, hair, and nails; iron, a mineral essential for healthy blood; and calcium, which helps promote strong bones.

When it comes to versatile, good-tasting, reasonably priced "health" foods, beans are hard to beat! Include beans as part of an overall varied diet low in fat and low to moderate in calories, and you will be taking giant steps on the road to good health.

WHAT IS A BEAN?

Beans are members of the *legume* family, which also includes certain peas, such as split and black-eyed. Technically speaking, legumes are plants that contain pods with seeds inside them. The word "legume" may describe the plant itself or the beans and peas they contain.

Popular members of the legume family include black beans, kidney beans, navy beans, lentils, soybeans, chickpeas (also known as garbanzo beans), and black-eyed peas. These and other legumes are highlighted in the recipes in this book, and are described in more detail later.

A few of the legumes, such as snap beans, mung beans, and fresh (not dry) lima beans, are really considered vegetables, and aren't included in *Bean Power*. While these beans are certainly valuable foods, they are not as rich in the fiber and other nutrients that make true legumes especially healthful.

WHY YOU NEED THIS BOOK

Despite their power-packed nutrient composition, until recently beans weren't accorded the respect they deserve in the American diet. Because they're inexpensive, and because they can cause gas when eaten in excess (more about ways to reduce gas later), we tended to look down our noses at these wholesome and hearty edibles.

No longer. In recent years, our attitude toward beans has been changing for the better, with the growing realization that beans—like vegetables, fruits, and grains—contain nutrients vital for good health and disease prevention.

Actually, we've basically rediscovered what people from diverse parts of the world have known for centuries. In Europe, the Near East, Asia, and Central and South America, people have built their diets around beans and grains for thousands of years. Now Americans are recognizing the nutritional and money-saving wisdom of doing the same.

Recent surveys suggest approximately 10 percent of Americans are eating more beans, vegetables, and grains —and less meat—than ever before. Four out of ten consumers say they have even changed their dining-out habits to reflect nutritional concerns. Not surprisingly, this new direction has prompted a virtual explosion of restaurants and fast-food outlets that serve a wide variety of ethnic, bean-based dishes such as chili, rice, and beans and fajitas.

Quick and Easy Meals

With this book, you can prepare many of the same tasty meals you enjoy when eating out—in minutes, right at home! Are you a chili lover? Try our hearty Two-Bean Chili (p. 51). Roll-Your-Own Fajitas, filled with meat, rice, beans, and salad fixings (p. 55). Or dip into a robust South-of-the-Border Black Bean Dip (p. 29)—the perfect, healthy accompaniment to raw veggies or chips.

Of course, *Bean Power* contains many other delicious recipes as well. In the Soups section, you'll find palate pleasers that do double duty as a first course or a light meal on their own. In a mere fifteen minutes, you can savor a delectable Chick-Pea and Watercress soup (p. 42). In even less time, you can prepare a lovely and wholesome White Bean Soup (p. 37)—and much more.

Main Dishes presents beans in all their glory. Try irresistible Yellow Split Pea Fritters with Roasted Red Pepper Sauce (p. 70); eye-catching, mouth-watering Shrimp and Asparagus with Gingered Bean Sauce (p. 58); or a richly satisfying Lentil Meat Loaf (p. 68).

Main Dish Salads include a delicious eight-minute marvel, Kidney Bean, Chicken, and Mango Salad (p. 93) and a continental favorite, Classic Italian White Bean and Tuna Salad (p. 94).

Pastas and the incredibly versatile bean also give these dishes a creative twist: flavorful Mexican Lasagne (p. 107), for instance, or healthful and tasty Spinach and Chick-Pea Shells (p. 105).

Salads and Side Dishes are next. Imagine immersing your fork in an Orangy Sweet Potato with Red and White Kidney Beans (p. 141) or a taste-tempting Mashed Split Peas and Potatoes (p. 132). Salad starters include a sweet and tangy Fruited Wild Rice and Bean Salad (p. 123) and a Middle East–style Crunchy Curried Yellow Split Pea, Brown Rice, and Apple Salad (p. 125).

Finally, our treats in the Sweets section: scrumptious Raspberry Almond Bean Pie is practically a meal unto itself (p. 151). For a lighter touch, top off your meal with Molasses Bean Soufflé with Lemon-Ginger Sauce (p. 153).

These remarkable dishes and many, many more in *Bean Power* will enrich your menus, tickle your taste buds, and add lots of good nutritional and life-lasting benefits to you and your family's diet in minutes!

BEANS BATTLE DISEASE

Enlisting beans to help fend off disease is one of the smartest dietary moves you can make. Here's a look at beans' exceptional health-promoting properties.

Beans Help Reduce Cancer Risks

Beans play several roles as cancer-fighters. As we've seen, they contain lots of fiber. According to the American Cancer Society, fiber functions in diverse ways that may reduce cancer risk. Fiber dilutes the contents of the colon, thus limiting contact between the lining of the colon and any carcinogens that may be present. Fiber also helps reduce the concentration of carcinogens and other cancer promoters, such as bile acids. And, in contrast to low fiber diets, diets high in fiber tend to be lower in calories and higher in vitamins and minerals, which can also exert a protective effect against cancer.

Beans contain very little fat—another plus in protecting against cancer. Some studies show a correlation between high dietary fat intake and cancers of the breast, colon, and prostate; these studies suggest fat may somehow promote tumor development. Other studies implicate excessive calories (easy to consume on a diet that contains lots of high-fat foods) as the culprit in the development of these and other cancers.

Either way, beans are winners: they're chock-full of nutrients, extremely low in fat, filling and satisfying, and they weigh in at an average of 230 calories per cup, cooked—making only a very modest contribution to your day's total calories.

Beans Help Protect Against Heart Disease

Beans aid in the fight against heart disease by helping to lower blood cholesterol levels and, again, reducing the amount of fat in our diet.

More than one in four Americans suffers from some form of cardiovascular disease, according to the American Heart Association. A major contributing factor to the development of heart disease is a high blood cholesterol level. Studies suggest that the fiber in beans—as well as in fruit, vegetables, and certain grains—can play a role in lowering blood cholesterol levels, thereby reducing the risk of heart disease (for details, see the section on Fiber, p. 9).

As part of an overall healthy diet low to moderate in calories, beans also help prevent heart disease by helping you maintain a desirable weight. Obesity is a major risk factor for heart disease.

Beans Help Manage Diabetes

Beans can play an important role in a diabetic diet because they're high in carbohydrates and fiber—both of which help keep blood sugar on an even keel.

According to the American Diabetes Association (ADA), 55 to 60 percent of a diabetic's calories should come from carbohydrates (the same as everyone else's), with simple carbohydrates (sugar) contributing no more than 5 percent of these calories. The ADA also recommends that a person with diabetes consume 35 to 40 grams of fiber daily—compared with a recommendation of 25 to 30 grams for a nondiabetic person.

Once again, beans fill the bill. As we saw earlier, beans contain large amounts of fiber. And from 60 to 75 percent of beans' calories come from carbohydrate, depending on the type of bean (the remaining calories come mainly from protein). Because of their high fiber and carbohydrate content, beans are now encouraged on a diabetic diet.

Beans Combat Overweight

Beans combat obesity for several reasons. First, they have a low caloric density—meaning you get lots of filling food and nutrition for relatively few calories. Beans' calories come largely from carbohydrates and protein, each of which contains *four* calories per gram. Fat, on the other hand, contains *nine* calories per gram. So foods high in fat are considered calorie *dense:* you get more calories, less satisfaction, and less nutrition per serving.

The high carbohydrate content of beans means that calories from beans are burned up by the body very quickly and converted into usable energy. This contrasts with calories from high-fat foods, which the body tends to store rather than use. There's also some evidence that burning calories from carbohydrates actually causes the body to burn even more calories, setting off a snowball-type effect. We'll explore how this works in more detail later.

The fiber in beans also assists in weight loss and maintenance. Fiber helps you feel "full" and, therefore, you'll be less likely to overeat during a meal (the effect is similar to drinking water before a meal to curb hunger). High-fiber foods also help the dieter because they require more chewing; this forces you to eat more slowly and, in all probability, consume less food than you would if you could simply gulp down your meal.

A CLOSER LOOK AT KEY NUTRIENTS

Fiber, complex carbohydrates, low-fat protein, and certain vitamins and minerals form the foundation of beans' contribution to good health. A closer look at these important nutrients reveals how they perform their nutritional magic.

Fiber

We've seen that the large amounts of fiber contained in beans help combat cancer and heart disease, manage diabetes, and assist in weight control. To gain a better understanding of how this is accomplished, it's important to know some facts about fiber and how it works in the body.

Fiber comes in two main forms: soluble and insoluble. Soluble fiber dissolves easily in water, forming a gummy, gluelike material. Insoluble fiber does not dissolve.

Plant foods contain both types of fiber but, depending on the plant, one type predominates. In beans, it's soluble fiber. The exact mechanism by which beans protect against cancer and heart disease isn't yet known. But it appears that soluble fiber's main health-promoting action is to remove bile acids—substances necessary for the digestion of fat—from the body. The prompt removal of bile acids from the body may help reduce the risk of cancer—particularly cancer of the colon—because when bile acids are eliminated they take potential carcinogens with them.

With respect to soluble fiber's role in helping to prevent heart disease, the picture is somewhat more complicated: The elimination of bile acids that become entangled in the gummy web of soluble fiber prompts the body to produce more bile acids for later use in fat digestion.

Cholesterol contains some of the chemical substances needed to produce bile acids. So, in order to produce more bile acids, the body must first remove some of the circulating cholesterol from the blood. The result: less cholesterol circulating in the blood—and a lowered risk of heart disease.

Dietary Fiber Content of Beans and Legumes	
	grams per ¹/₂ cup, cooked
Black beans	7.5
Black-eyed peas	4.6
Chick-peas	6.2
Kidney beans	6.1
Lentils	7.8
Lima beans	6.6
Navy beans	4.6
Pinto beans	7.3
Soybeans	5.2
Split peas	8.1
White beans	5.7

Complex Carbohydrates

Carbohydrates play a role in weight reduction and regulation of blood sugar levels. But not all carbohydrates are created equal.

Like fiber, carbohydrates come in two main forms: simple carbohydrates, found largely in table sugar and candy; and complex carbohydrates, found in beans and other starchy, high-fiber foods. Both forms are eventually broken down into glucose, the body's main fuel. So why choose complex carbohydrates over the simple ones?

For several good reasons. First, foods high in complex carbohydrates—beans, vegetables, fruits, grains—are also rich in other important vitamins and minerals necessary for health. Simple carbohydrate foods such as candy and cookies generally contain little in the way of nutrients.

As we've seen, complex carbohydrates have a low caloric density, meaning you get lots of nutrition—and a feeling of "fullness"—for relatively few calories. Therefore, complex carbohydrates are a boon for weight control. Simple carbohydrates, like fats, tend to be calorie dense: even small servings of simple carbohydrates contain relatively high amounts of calories and little else. For example, a half-cup serving of cooked beans—with its complex carbohydrates, fiber, protein, vitamins, and minerals—contains about the same number of calories as a roll of candy mints.

There are additional benefits to including plenty of complex carbohydrates in your diet. They help keep blood sugar on an even keel, which is important for diabetics and nondiabetics alike. A dramatic rise in blood sugar levels, which can occur after you eat a food high in simple carbohydrates, is generally followed by a precipitous *drop* in blood sugar levels. This results in energy highs and lows that can interfere with functioning. Complex carbohydrates, on the other hand, allow a relatively steady trickle of glucose into the blood after a meal, because it takes the body time to break them down and digest them.

The way in which carbohydrates are digested by the body also has a beneficial result. The body appears to expend more calories when digesting carbohydrates than it does in the digestion of fat. Therefore, carbohydrate foods are said to have a greater *thermic effect*—they cause more calories to be burned after eating—than high fat foods. It seems that 25 percent of excess carbohydrate calories are used up in the digestion and conversion of carbohydrates to body fat, whereas almost all of the excess fat calories we consume are immediately stored as body fat. So by eating foods high in carbohydrates—especially the complex kind—you actually give your body fewer calories to convert into fat.

Some studies suggest that the thermic effect stimulates the body to *continue* burning carbohydrates for as long as two hours after you've eaten a high-carbohydrate meal. No such effect occurs after consumption of a high-fat meal.

Protein

Protein, like oxygen, is essential to the proper functioning of every cell in the body. The brain, muscles, skin, hair, nails, and tissues that hold the body together are all made primarily of protein—and beans are an excellent source of this vital nutrient.

Protein, like fiber and carbohydrates, comes in two main forms: complete protein, found in animal foods such as meat, poultry, fish, and dairy products—and incomplete protein, found in beans, grains, and other plant foods. The amount and type of *amino acids* the protein contains determine whether it is complete or incomplete.

Amino acids are divided into two types: essential amino acids, which must be provided by the diet, and nonessential amino acids, which are produced by the body (but may also come from diet). Animal foods contain all the essential amino acids, and are therefore complete. Plant foods such as beans are deficient in one or more essential amino acids. Fortunately, however, all plant foods are not low in the same amino acids. By combining plant foods that are low in different essential amino acids, you can obtain adequate amounts of complete protein even if you don't eat animal foods. Two proteins that compensate for each other's deficiencies in this way are called *complementary proteins*.

Many of the recipes in this book include complementary proteins, such as the black-eyed peas and rice in Herbed Hoppin' John (p. 147) and the Brown Rice and Red Bean Pilaf (p. 145).

B Vitamins

Adequate amounts of B vitamins are vital for a strong immune system, high energy, healthy skin, hair, and nails, and the production of healthy blood cells. Beans are an excellent source of all the B vitamins (except vitamin B_{12}, which is only present in animal foods). In addition to fiber, complex carbohydrates, and protein, the B vitamins are a major nutritional plus for beans.

Iron

Beans are also an excellent source of iron, with anywhere from 3 to 6 milligrams per cup, cooked, depending on the variety of bean. Iron is vital for healthy red blood cells, and adequate amounts are needed to avoid the debilitating effects of iron-deficiency anemia.

There are two types of dietary iron: *heme* iron, the form found in animal foods, and *nonheme* iron, found in beans and other plant foods. Nonheme iron is not as easily absorbed by the body as heme iron. However, eating foods that contain nonheme iron with foods that contain vitamin C (such as fruits and vegetables), or with an animal food, makes nonheme iron more available. Most of the recipes in this book feature beans in combination with fruits or vegetables, meat, poultry, or fish.

Calcium

Calcium is vital for healthy bones and teeth, and also plays a role in keeping our immune system sound. Beans are a good source of calcium, providing between 50 and 130 milligrams per cup, depending on the type of bean. Soybeans contain the highest amounts of calcium among the members of the legume family.

OVERCOMING "GASSINESS"

Gassiness, technically known as flatulence, is a consequence of the digestion of certain types of sugars, called *oligosaccharides,* contained in beans. Although they can't be eliminated entirely, the amount of oligosaccharides in beans can be reduced during preparation and cooking.

Most food substances are digested in the stomach and small intestine, and remaining indigestible substances are sent into the large intestine for removal from the body. But the oligosaccharides in beans aren't digested in the stomach or small intestine; instead, they arrive intact in the large intestine, where they are digested by bacteria. The digestion process causes the beans to ferment, producing gas.

During preparation, you can reduce the amount of oligosaccharides in beans—and thereby reduce their gas-causing potential—by discarding the water you've used to soak beans and replacing that water with 3 or 4 cups of fresh water before cooking. If you're using shortcut methods of preparation—bringing cooking water to a boil and dropping legumes into the boiling water, or using a pressure cooker—then discard the cooking water from the pot or pressure cooker halfway through and resume cooking with fresh water. A pinch of baking soda to the cooking water will also reduce the gassiness sometimes caused by beans. Commercial preparations such as Beano to improve bean digestion may also be purchased at health food stores.

GETTING TO KNOW BEANS

Legumes are probably the oldest form of food known to mankind, and many different varieties are grown around the world. Here's a look at the more popular beans and peas in the American diet, which are included in *Bean Power*.

Black Beans

These sweet-tasting beans are thick and hearty—perfect for soups and salads. For a delicious, south-of-the-border treat, try our Black Bean Soup (p. 47) or our Black Bean, Avocado, and Yellow Rice Salad (p. 91).

Black-eyed Peas

These tasty peas—white with a black spot on the side—are the main ingredient of the popular dish, Herbed Hoppin' John (p. 147). One of several varieties of cowpeas, black-eyed peas thrive in a warm climate and are an important food throughout the Southern states.

Chick-Peas (Garbanzos)

These yellow peas have a hazelnut shape and size, and a delicate, nutty flavor. They're popular in Middle Eastern–style dishes, such as Hummus (p. 33) and Moroccan-style Chick-Pea and Vegetable Couscous Casserole (p. 80).

Kidney Beans

These versatile red or white kidney-shaped beans have a firm skin, but are tender and sweet inside. They're the main ingredient in many Mexican dishes, including our Vegetable Bean Enchiladas (p. 53) and Refried Beans (p. 129)

Lentils

These tan or red, small disk-shape beans are terrific for soups, salads, and dishes that require a thick, "meaty" texture. Try our Lentil Soup (p. 43), Lentil Meat Loaf (p. 68), or Lentil and Orange Salad (p. 122).

Lima Beans

Lima beans have the unusual distinction of being both a bean (in its dried, white form) and a vegetable (when fresh and green). They're native to the Americas and were grown by the Indians for centuries before the arrival of Columbus. The name "Lima" comes from the city of Lima, capital of Peru, where early explorers from Europe first discovered this bean.

For an unusual side dish, try our Lima Beans with Lemon and Poppy Seeds (p. 135).

Navy Beans

Navy beans are white with an oval shape and have a sweet, delicate flavor. They're popular baked, and in salads and casseroles. Try our Light-style Baked Beans with Ham (p. 74), White Bean and Watercress Salad with Tomato Dressing (p. 119), or Pasta and Vegetables with Cheesy White Bean Sauce (p. 103).

Pinto Beans

These beige or speckled beans have a delicate flavor. Like the kidney bean, they're a favorite ingredient in chilis and salads. Try our Curried Pinto Bean Dip (p. 30) and our Pinto Bean Salad with Ham (p. 116).

Soybeans

Soybeans have a delicate flavor, and are often used as a meat substitute. Of all the legumes, they have the most complete protein—similar to the protein found in meat. Try our hearty Two-Bean Chili (p. 51), or crunchy Soybean Granola (p. 157) at breakfast or snack time.

Split Peas

These yellow or green peas complement just about any type of dish, including our Split Pea and Spinach Soup (p. 39) and our Crunchy Curried Yellow Split Pea, Brown Rice, and Apple Salad (p. 125).

BUYING GUIDE

Packaged dried beans provide a world of healthful nutrients for just pennies per serving. Even canned beans, which cost more per serving than dried beans, are a terrific nutritional bargain. You get ample amounts of protein, fiber, vitamins, and minerals for a fraction of the cost of animal foods. And what you *don't* get counts, too— no cholesterol, and very small amounts of fat.

- For best taste and nutrition, buy beans as soon as possible after packaging. Shop in stores that have a rapid turnover of goods; try different outlets and brands.

- Look for firm, clean beans with no visible dirt or small stones.

- Beans should be similar in size and color; otherwise, they will cook unevenly.

- Make sure bags are strong and well sealed, with no punctures or openings.

- If buying beans loose from a bin, sift through and select beans with a fresh appearance. Avoid beans with tiny pinholes, which can be a sign of bug infestation.

- If buying canned beans, check the freshness date.

STORAGE TIPS

- Store beans in their plastic bags until ready for use. After opening, transfer remaining beans to glass jars with tight-fitting lids and store in a cool, dry place.

- Never mix different types of beans or older beans with new ones; they all require different soaking and cooking times.

- Beans can be stored for years, but are best if used within six to nine months of purchase.

- Keep cooked beans tightly covered in the refrigerator for use within five days.

Ready for an adventure in the delightful world of bean cookery? Turn the page to learn how to prepare beans— and cook them to perfection!

BEAN BASICS

HOW TO SOAK AND COOK DRIED BEANS

Soaking and cooking dried beans is neither difficult nor complicated. Use either soaking method outlined below and cook the beans for the necessary amount of time for that particular bean. Lentils, split peas, and black-eyed peas do not need to be soaked, but other beans do. Many recipes can be made with canned beans, however I generally prefer soaked dried beans unless I'm in a real hurry. If you choose to use canned beans, be sure to rinse and drain them before using them in the recipe.

Quick-Soaking Method:
1. Rinse and pick over dried beans. Place beans and three times their volume of hot water in a saucepan. Bring the beans to a boil and boil for 2 minutes.

2. Remove the saucepan from heat and allow the beans to soak for 1 hour. Drain and rinse the beans before cooking.

Traditional Soaking Method:
1. Rinse and pick over dried beans. Place beans and three times their volume of hot water in a bowl.

2. Allow beans to soak for 4 hours or overnight. They will not absorb much more water than can be absorbed in 4 hours, but you may soak longer for convenience. (Soybeans will need the full 12 hours of soaking.) Change the soaking water a few times during soaking. This will help to break down the indigestible sugars that can lead to flatulence.

3. Drain and rinse the beans before cooking.

How to Cook Beans:
Cooking time:

Adzuki	1–1$^1/_2$ hours
Black Beans	1$^1/_2$ hours
Black-Eyed Peas	1 hour
Cannelini (White Kidney) Beans	1 hour
Chick-Peas	2–2$^1/_2$ hours
Great Northern Beans	1$^1/_2$ hours
Kidney (red) Beans	1$^1/_2$ hours
Lentils	30–35 minutes
Lima Beans	1–1$^1/_2$ hours
Navy Beans	2 hours
Pigeon Peas	30 minutes
Pink Beans	1–1$^1/_2$ hours
Pinto Beans	1–1$^1/_2$ hours
Red Beans	1–1$^1/_2$ hours
Small White Beans	2 hours
Split Peas	30 minutes
Soybeans	3–3$^1/_2$ hours

Yield: 1 pound dry beans = 2 cups dry = 5–6 cups cooked

Cooking Beans:
1. Place soaked beans in a large saucepan. Cover with three times their volume of water. Add herbs or spices as desired. Do not add salt or acidic ingredients such as vinegar, tomatoes, or juice, which substantially slow the cooking. Add these ingredients when the beans are just tender.

2. Bring to a boil, lower heat, and simmer gently, stirring occasionally until tender. Do not boil the beans or their skins will break. Cooking times vary with the type

of beans used, but may also vary with the age of the beans. Beans are done when they can be easily mashed between two fingers, or with a fork. Always test a few beans in case they are unevenly cooked.

3. Rinse and drain.

HOW TO SPROUT BEANS

Adzuki, lentils, soybeans, and even chick-peas can be sprouted. Try sprouting with all the different varieties.

Yield: 2 to 3 tablespoons dry beans = $1^1/_2$ cups sprouts

1. Soak beans by traditional method (see p. 23). Drain.

2. Place the beans in a glass jar. Cover the jar with a double layer of cheesecloth, secured with a rubber band.

3. Rinse the beans twice daily, for 4 or 5 days, draining water through the cheesecloth. Be sure to drain the beans well each time. Remove the unsprouted beans and serve sprouts with or as a salad, with your favorite dressing.

DIPS AND SPREADS

South-of-the-Border Black Bean Dip

Try this healthy dip at your next party. Serve it with fresh salsa and salt-free tortilla chips.

Preparation time: 2 minutes
Cooking time: 1 minute
Makes 1 cup

2 teaspoons ground cumin
2 cups cooked black beans
2 tablespoons chopped green bell pepper
2 tablespoons chopped red bell pepper
1 tablespoon olive oil
2 teaspoons cider vinegar
1 tablespoon minced jalapeño pepper
Freshly ground black pepper
Salt, to taste

1. In a small skillet, heat cumin over very low flame, just until fragrant, about 1 minute.

2. Combine cumin and remaining ingredients in a food processor. Process until smooth. Serve with tortilla chips.

CURRIED PINTO BEAN DIP

Serve this dip with crudités or try stuffing it in the whites of hard-cooked eggs for an interesting appetizer. One cup of the dip will fill about 16 egg-white halves.

Preparation time: 3 minutes
Cooking time: 1 minute
Makes 1 cup

1 tablespoon curry powder
$^{1}/_{4}$ teaspoon ground cinnamon
$^{1}/_{2}$ teaspoon powdered turmeric
2 cups cooked pinto beans
2 tablespoons cider vinegar
1 tablespoon vegetable oil
$^{1}/_{2}$ teaspoon grated orange zest
Salt, to taste

1. In a small skillet, heat curry powder, cinnamon, and turmeric over very low flame, just until fragrant, about 1 minute.

2. Combine pinto beans, vinegar, oil, orange zest, and salt in a food processor. Add spices. Process until smooth. Serve with fresh vegetables.

GINGERED WHITE BEAN DIP

This is a perfect dip for a summer gathering. Serve it with fresh, crisp vegetable sticks.

Preparation time: 5 minutes
Cooking time: None
Makes 1 cup

  2 cups cooked white beans
  1 tablespoon grated ginger
  4 teaspoons extra-virgin olive oil
  1 tablespoon honey
  1 tablespoon cider vinegar
  $^1/_2$ teaspoon mustard powder
  Pinch white pepper
  Salt, to taste
  Water
  2 teaspoons chopped chives

1. Combine beans, ginger, oil, honey, vinegar, mustard powder, white pepper, and salt in a food processor. Process until smooth, adding water tablespoon by tablespoon, as necessary.

2. Stir in chives and serve with crisp vegetable sticks.

LENTIL AND ONION COMPOTE

This wonderful, naturally sweet spread is delicious on crusty French bread. Serve it as an hors d'oeuvre, an appetizer, or with lunch.

Preparation time: 5 minutes
Cooking time: 65 to 70 minutes
Makes 1¹/₄ cups

> **2 cups diced onions**
> **1 tablespoon olive oil**
> **1 cup, plus 2 tablespoons water**
> **1 cup cooked lentils**
> **2 tablespoons sherry**
> **¹/₂ teaspoon salt, or to taste**
> **¹/₂ teaspoon freshly ground black pepper**

1. In a medium heavy-bottom saucepan, combine onion, oil, and 2 tablespoons water. Cook over medium heat, stirring occasionally, until onion is just golden, 10 to 15 minutes.

2. Add lentils and remaining water, cover, and cook over very low heat for 1 hour, stirring occasionally.

3. Stir in sherry, salt, and pepper and cook uncovered until compote is thick.

# HUMMUS

Serve this traditional Middle Eastern dip with toasted whole wheat pita triangles. Tahini paste should be available in the Oriental foods section of your supermarket or at the health food store.

Preparation time: 5 minutes
Cooking time: None
Makes 1¹/₂ cups

   2 cups cooked chick-peas
   ³/₄ cup lemon juice
   ¹/₃ cup tahini (sesame seed) paste
   3 cloves garlic, chopped
   ¹/₂ teaspoon salt, or to taste

1. Combine all ingredients in a food processor. Process until smooth or to desired consistency.

SOUPS

 **WHITE BEAN SOUP**

This is a perfect, pure white bean soup. Purée more or less of the beans to taste.

Preparation time: 2 minutes
Cooking time: 10 minutes
Serves 6

3 tablespoons extra-virgin olive oil
2 cloves garlic, minced
5¹/₂ cups cooked white beans, any variety
3 tablespoons chopped parsley
¹/₂ teaspoon freshly ground black pepper
1¹/₂ cups chicken stock, reduced-sodium chicken
    broth, water or broth/water combination
Salt, to taste

Garnish:

2 tablespoons finely chopped parsley
1 teaspoon grated lemon zest,
¹/₄ teaspoon freshly ground black pepper

1. In a large (12-inch) nonstick skillet or saucepan, heat oil over medium flame. Add garlic and cook, stirring until tender. Add beans, parsley, and pepper. Stir to coat, add stock and salt, cover, and simmer for 10 minutes. Cool slightly.

(*Continued on next page*)

2. Transfer 1^1/$_2$ cups of the beans to a food processor. Process until smooth and return to skillet. Stir soup and heat through.

3. To prepare garnish: Combine parsley, lemon zest, and pepper. Ladle soup into bowls and sprinkle with garnish.

Split Pea and Spinach Soup

I have been making this soup for years and have no idea where the recipe originally came from. It's one of my all-time favorites for a winter lunch.

Preparation time: 3 minutes
Cooking time: 2 to 2¹/₂ hours
Serves 6

    2 tablespoons vegetable oil
    1 cup chopped onion
    1 clove garlic, minced
    1 tablespoon whole mustard seeds
    1¹/₂ teaspoons powdered turmeric
    1 pound dried split peas
    5 cups chicken stock, reduced-sodium chicken broth, water or a stock/water combination
    5 cups water
    ¹/₂ teaspoon salt
    1 10-ounce package frozen chopped spinach, defrosted and drained
    ¹/₄ cup lemon juice, or to taste
    Salt, to taste
    Freshly ground black pepper, to taste

1. In a large (4-quart) wide saucepan, heat oil over medium flame. Add onion, garlic, mustard seeds, and turmeric. Cook, stirring until onions are tender and mustard seeds begin to pop.

(Continued on next page)

2. Stir in peas, stock, water, and salt. Bring mixture to a boil, reduce heat and simmer, uncovered, stirring occasionally, until peas have disintegrated, 2 to $2^{1/2}$ hours.

3. Add spinach and lemon juice, season with salt and pepper, heat through, and serve.

PASTA E FAGIOLI

This is a light and colorful version of the classic Italian soup.

Preparation time: 10 minutes
Cooking time: 15 minutes
Serves 6

**4 cups chicken stock or reduced-sodium chicken
    broth
2 cups water
1 cup small pasta, such as ditalini
2 cups cooked kidney beans
2 ounces fresh green beans, cut in $^1/_2$-inch pieces
1 cup tomato, seeded and diced
$^1/_2$ cup corn kernels
$^1/_2$ cup finely diced carrot
$^1/_4$ cup chopped fresh dill
1 tablespoon white vinegar
Salt, to taste
Freshly ground black pepper, to taste**

1. In a large saucepan, combine broth and water. Bring to a boil. Add pasta and cook for 5 minutes.

2. Add kidney and green beans, tomato, corn kernels, and carrot, and simmer until pasta is tender. Stir in dill and vinegar and add salt and pepper to taste.

CHICK-PEA AND WATERCRESS SOUP

If you make this soup with canned chick-peas it's a snap! It is also a very impressive-tasting first course or light meal.

Preparation time: 10 minutes
Cooking time: 5 minutes
Serves 6

> 3 cups chopped onion
> 3 teaspoons vegetable oil
> 9 cups cooked chick-peas
> 3 teaspoons fresh or ¹/₄ teaspoon dried sage
> ³/₄ teaspoon freshly ground black pepper
> 9 cups chicken stock or reduced-sodium chicken
>   broth
> 6 tablespoons lemon juice
> 6 cups packed, coarsely chopped watercress
> 9 tablespoons chopped parsley

1. In a medium saucepan, heat oil over medium flame. Add onion and cook, stirring, until tender. Add chick-peas, sage, and pepper. Toss to coat.

2. Add stock and lemon juice and heat mixture just to boiling. Remove from heat, and cool slightly. Transfer mixture to a food processor and process until smooth.

3. Return chick-pea mixture to saucepan. Add watercress and parsley and heat until watercress is just wilted. Serve promptly.

🫘 LENTIL SOUP

This is a wonderful classic lentil soup. Use stock for a rich flavor, water or vegetable stock for a lighter touch.

Preparation time: 10 minutes
Cooking time: 45 to 50 minutes
Serves 8 to 10

   3 tablespoons olive oil
   1 cup chopped onion
   1 cup chopped carrot
   1 cup finely chopped celery
   4 cloves garlic, minced
   $^1/_4$ cup chopped parsley
   1 teaspoon dried thyme
   $^1/_4$ teaspoon ground cumin
   1 bay leaf
   2 cups dried lentils
   4 cups chicken or beef stock, reduced-sodium
      chicken or beef broth or water
   4 cups water
   Tabasco or other hot sauce, to taste
   Salt, to taste
   Lemon or lime wedges

1. Heat oil in a large (4 to 6 quart) saucepan over medium-low flame. Add onions and cook, stirring, until tender. Add carrots, celery, and garlic and cook until golden, about 5 minutes.

(*Continued on next page*)

2. Stir lentils, parsley, thyme, cumin, and bay leaf into onion mixture until well coated. Add stock and bring mixture to a boil. Reduce heat and gently simmer soup until lentils are soft, 35 to 45 minutes. Cool slightly.

3. Remove bay leaf and discard. Transfer 2 cups of lentils to a food processor. Process until smooth and return to saucepan. Heat soup through and season with Tabasco and salt. Garnish with lemon or lime wedges.

MINESTRONE

Minestrone literally means "big soup." Serve this one with a thick slice of multigrain bread.

Preparation time: 10 minutes
Cooking time: 45 minutes
Serves 6

   2 tablespoons olive oil
   1 cup thinly sliced onion
   4 cloves garlic, minced
   $3/4$ cup diced carrots
   $3/4$ cup diced celery
   1 14-ounce can Italian plum tomatoes, diced,
      including juice
   $2^1/2$ cups chicken or beef stock, reduced-sodium
      chicken or beef broth, water or broth/water
      combination
   $1^1/2$ cups shredded red cabbage
   3 tablespoons chopped fresh basil
   3 tablespoons chopped fresh parsley
   $3/4$ teaspoon dried thyme
   $3/4$ teaspoon dried oregano
   3 cups cooked pinto, navy or Great Northern beans
   $2^1/2$ cups diced zucchini
   Salt, to taste
   Grated Parmesan cheese
   Freshly ground black pepper, to taste

1. Heat oil in a large (4-quart) saucepan over medium
   flame. Add onions and cook, stirring until tender. Add

garlic, carrots, and celery and cook until onions are golden.

2. Stir in tomatoes, stock, cabbage, basil, parsley, thyme, and oregano. Bring to a boil, reduce heat and simmer for 30 minutes, stirring occasionally.

3. Add beans and zucchini and simmer for 15 minutes. Add salt to taste. Serve with grated Parmesan cheese and freshly ground black pepper.

BLACK BEAN SOUP

Welcome to South America! This light version of Black Bean Soup leaves out the fat of the traditional ham bone or salt pork. But you can serve it with just a sprinkle of chopped ham to give a little of that smoky pork flavor.

Preparation time: 5 minutes
Cooking time: 1^1/$_2$ to 2 hours
Serves 6 to 7

2 tablespoons olive oil
^{1}/$_2$ cup chopped onion
^{1}/$_2$ cup chopped red bell pepper
^{1}/$_2$ cup chopped green bell pepper
2 cloves garlic, minced
1 small jalapeño pepper
1 teaspoon ground cumin
1 teaspoon oregano
Pinch ground cloves
1 pound dried black beans, soaked
6 cups beef stock or reduced-sodium beef broth
^{1}/$_2$ cup dry sherry
1 teaspoon reduced-sodium soy sauce, or to taste

1. In a large (4-quart) saucepan, heat oil, onions, peppers, and garlic over medium flame. Cook, stirring, until onions are tender. Add cumin, oregano, and cloves and cook for 2 minutes.

2. Stir in beans and stock. Bring mixture to a boil, reduce heat, and simmer, uncovered, until beans are very soft. Add sherry and soy sauce and simmer for 20 minutes.

⬤ MINTED SPLIT AND FRESH PEA SOUP

I have been making a fresh pea soup for years, but here is a protein-rich version using split peas, as well. This fresh and delicious soup can be served hot, but is especially wonderful served chilled in the summer.

Preparation time: 3 minutes
Cooking time: 35 to 40 minutes
Serves 4 to 5

³/₄ cup dried split peas
3 cups water
1 10-ounce package frozen peas, thawed
3 tablespoons chopped fresh mint
¹/₂ teaspoon salt, or to taste
Pinch freshly ground black pepper

1. Place split peas and water in a saucepan over medium heat. Simmer until tender, about 30 minutes. Add frozen peas and continue simmering until they are cooked, 6 to 7 minutes. Cool slightly.

2. Place peas, water, mint, salt, and pepper in a food processor. Process until smooth. Serve hot or chill and serve.

MAIN DISHES

TWO-BEAN CHILI

If chili served over rice is the perfect winter meal, could chili made with soybeans be more than perfect? Soybeans have the highest protein content of any bean. Here's to your health!

Preparation time: 10 minutes
Cooking time: 50 minutes
Serves 8

  2 tablespoons vegetable oil
  1 cup chopped onion
  3 cloves garlic, minced
  1 cup diced carrot
  1 1/2 tablespoons chili powder
  1 teaspoon ground cumin
  1/2 teaspoon cayenne pepper
  1 teaspoon ground allspice
  2 28-ounce cans plum tomatoes, including juice
  3 cups cooked soybeans, chopped in a food
     processor
  2 cups cooked kidney beans
  2 teaspoons dijon mustard
  1 teaspoon salt, or to taste
  Freshly ground pepper, to taste

1. In a large saucepan, heat oil over medium flame. Add onion and cook, stirring, until translucent. Add garlic and carrot and continue cooking until onions are

golden. Stir in chili powder, cumin, cayenne, and all-spice and cook for 1 minute.

2. Stir in tomatoes and simmer for five minutes, breaking up the whole tomatoes with a spoon. Stir in beans and continue cooking until thickened, about 45 minutes.

3. Stir in mustard and season to taste with salt and pepper. Serve with chopped onion and a dollop of low-fat yogurt.

VEGETABLE BEAN ENCHILADAS

These enchiladas are simply delicious! Light, fresh tasting and so easy to make, serve them with rice for a great meal.

Preparation time: 15 minutes
Cooking time: 40 to 45 minutes
Serves 4 to 6

1 28-ounce can crushed tomatoes
1¹/₂ teaspoon chili powder
1 teaspoon ground cumin
¹/₃ cup water
1 tablespoon vegetable or olive oil
1 cup diced onion
2 cloves garlic, minced
1 cup diced red bell pepper
1 cup diced green bell pepper
2 cups chopped broccoli, steamed to crisp-tender
1 cup diced tomatoes, juice reserved
Salt, to taste
Freshly ground black pepper, to taste
10 flour tortillas
1 recipe refried beans (see p. 129)
1 cup shredded reduced-fat cheddar cheese

1. Preheat oven to 375°F. In a small saucepan, combine crushed tomatoes, water, chili powder, and cumin. Bring to a boil, reduce heat, cover, and simmer for 10 minutes. Set aside. (*Continued on next page*)

2. Meanwhile, heat oil in a large nonstick skillet, over medium flame. Add onion and cook, stirring until tender, about 3 minutes. Add peppers, broccoli, and garlic and continue cooking until peppers are tender, another 5 minutes. Add tomatoes and reserved juice and $1/4$ cup water, cover and cook for 4 minutes.

3. Divide the refried beans and spread evenly down the center of each of the 10 tortillas. Top each with some of the vegetable mixture, and sprinkle with 1 tablespoon of cheese.

4. Roll enchiladas and place, seam side down, side by side in a shallow baking dish. Leave $1/2$ inch between each. Top with sauce and sprinkle with remaining cheese.

5. Bake for 30 minutes. Serve with rice.

 ROLL-YOUR-OWN FAJITAS

Perfect for an easy and healthy party! Serve meat, rice and beans, vegetables, lettuce, sauce, and tortillas on separate serving platters and let everyone roll their own. For a lighter choice, try replacing the traditional tortillas with lettuce leaves!

Preparation time: 15 minutes, plus marination time
Cooking time: 30 minutes
Serves 7 to 8

> **14 to 16 flour tortillas**
> **1¹/₂ pounds flank steak or boneless chicken breasts**
> **¹/₄ head iceberg lettuce, finely shredded**

Marinade:

> **¹/₄ cup lime juice**
> **2 tablespoons grated ginger**
> **1 tablespoon olive oil**
> **4 dashes Tabasco sauce**

Sauce:

> **2 cups plain low-fat yogurt**
> **¹/₂ cup chopped cilantro**
> **2 cloves garlic, minced**

Rice and beans:

> **3 cups cooked black beans**
> **3 cups cooked brown rice**

(*Continued on next page*)

1 tablespoon olive oil
1 large onion, chopped
2 cloves garlic, minced
1 teaspoon ground cumin
1^1/$_2$ teaspoons chili powder
1 35-ounce can tomatoes, drained and coarsely
  chopped

Vegetables:

1^1/$_2$ tablespoons olive oil
2 red peppers, cored and cut in long strips
2 green peppers, cored and cut in long strips
2 medium zucchini, sliced ^{1}/$_4$-inch thick
2 yellow squash, sliced ^{1}/$_4$-inch thick
Salt, to taste
Freshly ground black pepper, to taste

1. Place beef or chicken in a shallow nonmetal baking dish. Mix together marinade ingredients and pour over meat. Leave for 1 hour.

2. Mix together sauce ingredients. Refrigerate until needed.

3. To prepare rice and beans: Heat 1 tablespoon oil in a heavy-bottom, 4-quart saucepan over medium flame. Add onions and cook until translucent, stirring frequently. Add garlic and spices and cook for 1 minute, stirring constantly.

4. Add tomatoes, and simmer for 3 minutes. Add rice and beans. Stir. Add pepper and salt to taste. Set aside.

5. To prepare vegetables: Heat 1 1/2 tablespoons of oil in a large skillet. Add vegetables and sauté until tender. Season with salt and pepper to taste.

6. Place steak or chicken on a broiler rack. Broil one side until nicely browned. Turn meat, brush with marinade, and continue cooking. Chicken should be cooked through, about 8 minutes. Allow meat to rest for 2 minutes before cutting.

7. Slice meat on a strong diagonal. Arrange platters on the table and instruct your guests to roll a little bit of everything in their tortillas and eat them with their hands.

SHRIMP AND ASPARAGUS WITH GINGERED BEAN SAUCE

Beans take on other flavors beautifully. Here, shrimp and asparagus are tossed with a lovely bean sauce enhanced with sweet and pungent flavors.

Preparation time: 5 minutes
Cooking time: 5 minutes
Serves 4

> 1 pound asparagus, stems trimmed and peeled, cut into 2-inch lengths
> 2 cups cooked Great Northern beans
> 1 tablespoon, plus 1 teaspoon grated ginger
> 1 tablespoon cider vinegar
> 1 tablespoon orange juice
> $1/4$ teaspoon freshly ground black pepper
> Pinch nutmeg
> Salt, to taste
> 1 tablespoon olive oil
> 1 pound large shrimp, peeled and deveined
> 2 tablespoons slivered fresh basil leaves

1. Blanch asparagus in boiling water until crisp-tender, about 2 minutes.

2. In a food processor, combine beans, 1 tablespoon ginger, vinegar, orange juice, pepper, nutmeg, and salt. Process until smooth, adding more orange juice, tablespoon by tablespoon, as necessary until sauce reaches desired consistency. Set aside.

3. In a large nonstick skillet, heat oil and 1 teaspoon ginger, over medium-high flame. Add shrimp and asparagus and cook for 1 minute. Quickly add white bean purée and toss with shrimp and asparagus. Cook until shrimp turn pink. Toss with basil and serve with brown rice.

WHITE BEAN RISOTTO WITH SHRIMP

This dish is an interesting twist on the classic risotto. It uses regular long-grain rice instead of short-grain arborio and does not have to be constantly stirred. The best surprise, however, is the addition of the beans which are a wonderful complement, especially in terms of nutrition.

Preparation time: 5 minutes
Cooking time: 25 to 30 minutes
Serves 5 to 6

3¹/₂ cups chicken stock or reduced-sodium chicken
    broth
2 teaspoons olive oil
¹/₄ cup chopped onion
1 cup long grain white rice
2 cups cooked white beans
3 tablespoons lemon juice
2 teaspoons lemon zest
1 pound shrimp, cleaned and peeled
1 cup packed watercress leaves
1 teaspoon fresh thyme leaves
Freshly ground black pepper, to taste

1. Heat broth to boiling. Lower heat and simmer.

2. In a large saucepan, combine oil and onion and cook until onion is tender. Add rice and stir to coat.

3. Add 1 cup of the hot broth, stir, cover, and simmer over a very low heat for 5 minutes. Add 1 more cup of

broth and beans, stir, cover, and simmer for another 10 minutes.

4. Add $1/2$ cup broth, lemon juice, and zest. Cook, stirring until broth is absorbed. Continue stirring and adding broth, $1/2$ cup at a time, making sure that liquid is absorbed between each addition, until rice is just tender. If you run out of stock, continue cooking with water.

5. Stir in shrimp, watercress, thyme, and pepper and cook, stirring, until the shrimp are pink. Serve promptly.

BROILED SALMON ON LEMONY WHITE BEAN PURÉE

This bean purée is heavenly. It can be served as a side dish or topped with a perfectly cooked piece of fish, as in this recipe.

Preparation time: 10 minutes, plus marination time
Cooking time: 10 to 15 minutes
Serves 4

> 4 salmon fillets, about ¹/₃ pound each
> 1 tablespoon chopped parsley, for garnish

Marinade:

> ¹/₂ cup white wine
> 2 tablespoons olive oil
> 2 tablespoons lemon juice
> ¹/₂ teaspoon salt
> ¹/₂ teaspoon dried thyme
> ¹/₄ teaspoon dried sage
> ¹/₄ teaspoon dried basil
> 1 tablespoon chopped parsley

Bean purée:

> 3 cups cooked cannelini beans
> ¹/₄ cup lemon juice
> 1 tablespoon lemon zest
> 2 teaspoons butter, melted
> 2 teaspoons vegetable or extra-virgin olive oil

Salt, to taste
$^1/_2$ teaspoon freshly ground black pepper

1. Place fish in a shallow, nonmetal baking dish. Whisk together the marinade ingredients. Pour over fish and allow it to marinate for 1 to 2 hours.

2. Broil fish until lightly browned on top, turn, and cook it until fork-tender, 10 to 15 minutes, depending on thickness.

3. Meanwhile, place beans, lemon juice and zest, butter, oil, salt, and pepper in a food processor. Purée until smooth.

4. Divide purée on individual serving plates. Place fish on top of purée and spoon remaining juices over it. Sprinkle with fresh chopped parsley. Serve promptly.

GINGERED CHICKEN AND CHICK-PEA CURRY

The chick-pea is the most common legume in Indian cuisine. Here is a very simple chicken curry.

Preparation time: 5 minutes
Cooking time: 70 to 75 minutes
Serves 4

3 cloves garlic, minced
1-inch cube ginger, peeled and diced
3 tablespoons water
2 tablespoons vegetable oil
$^1/_2$ cup chopped onion
1 tablespoon curry powder
1 pound skinned and boned chicken breasts, diced
1 tablespoon flour
3 cups chicken stock or reduced-sodium chicken broth
3 cups cooked chick-peas
$^1/_2$ cup tomato, peeled, seeded, and diced
3 tablespoons chopped parsley or cilantro
Salt, to taste
Freshly ground black pepper, to taste

1. Place garlic, ginger, and water in a food processor. Process until smooth.

2. In a large (4-quart) wide saucepan, heat oil over medium flame. Add onion and curry powder and cook, stirring, until onion is tender, about 3 minutes. Toss chicken pieces in flour. Shake off any excess. Increase

heat, add floured chicken pieces and cook until just browned on all sides.

3. Add garlic and ginger purée and stock and gently simmer for 45 minutes, uncovered. Stir in chick-peas, tomatoes, and parsley or cilantro and cook until chicken is fork-tender, about 25 minutes. Season with pepper and salt and serve over rice.

🫘 MEXICAN PIE

My family loves this dish. It is hearty, healthy, and full of nutritious ingredients.

Preparation time: 10 minutes
Cooking time: 65 to 70 minutes
Serves 6

2 cups cornmeal
1 teaspoon salt
5 cups water
1¼ cups shredded reduced-calorie cheddar cheese
2 tablespoons thinly sliced chives
¼ cup finely diced red bell peppers
Freshly ground black pepper, to taste
2 tablespoons olive or vegetable oil
1 cup chopped onion
1½ cups diced carrot
2 cloves garlic, minced
1½ pounds ground beef or turkey
2½ tablespoons chili powder
2 teaspoons ground cumin
1 14-ounce can plum tomatoes, with juice
3 cups cooked kidney beans
½ cup frozen peas, defrosted

1. Preheat oven to 350°F.

2. In a medium saucepan, stir together cornmeal, water, and salt. Heat mixture over a medium-low flame, stirring, until very thick, about 20 minutes. Stir 1 cup of

the cheese, red pepper, chives, and black pepper into mixture.

3. Meanwhile, heat oil in a large, nonstick skillet or wide saucepan, over medium flame. Add onion and cook, stirring until tender, 3 minutes. Add carrot and garlic and continue cooking until onion is golden.

4. Add ground beef or turkey, chili powder, and cumin. Cook, stirring and breaking up meat until browned. Add tomatoes and beans, bring mixture to a boil, reduce heat and simmer for 10 minutes, stirring occasionally. Stir in peas and heat through.

5. Line bottom and sides of a 2-quart casserole with $1/2$ of the cornmeal mixture. Fill casserole with meat and bean mixture. Dot top of casserole with remaining cornmeal mixture and sprinkle with remaining cheese. Bake until casserole is bubbly, about 30 minutes.

LENTIL MEAT LOAF

Here is a healthful alternative to an American classic. By adding lentils to this meat loaf it becomes much higher in fiber and lower in fat, without sacrificing any flavor. An added bonus, this version will fit even the tightest budget!

Preparation time: 10 minutes
Cooking time: 50 minutes
Serves 4 to 5

1 tablespoon olive oil
1¹/₂ cups chopped onion
1 cup grated carrot
2 cloves garlic, minced
1¹/₂ cups water
1 teaspoon dried thyme
1 teaspoon ground cumin
1 teaspoon dried rosemary
1 teaspoon salt
¹/₄ teaspoon nutmeg
³/₄ pound ground beef
1 egg, lightly beaten
¹/₄ cup chopped parsley
1 tablespoon tiny capers
3 cups cooked lentils
1¹/₂ cups cooked rice
2 tablespoons mustard

1. Preheat oven to 350°F.

2. Heat oil in a large nonstick skillet over medium flame. Add onion, carrot, and garlic. Cook, stirring until onion is golden. Stir in water, thyme, cumin, rosemary, salt, and nutmeg.

3. In a large bowl combine beef, egg, parsley, and capers, mixing with hands. Add lentils, rice, and vegetable mixture and mix gently until well combined.

4. Press mixture into a loaf pan and spread surface with mustard. Cover with aluminum foil and bake for 30 minutes. Remove foil and bake another 15 minutes. Allow the meat loaf to rest for 15 minutes before cutting.

🫘 YELLOW SPLIT PEA FRITTERS WITH ROASTED RED PEPPER SAUCE

This is an unusual, delicious use for split peas. The accompanying red pepper sauce will soon become a favorite.

Preparation time: 5 minutes, plus 1 hour refrigeration
Cooking time: 25 to 30 minutes, for fritters; 50 minutes,
   for sauce
Serves 4 to 5

   1 cup yellow split peas, cooked tender
   ¹/₄ cup bread crumbs
   1 egg
   2 tablespoons low-fat milk
   2 teaspoons olive oil
   1 cup chopped onion
   ¹/₂ cup chopped red pepper
   ¹/₂ cup chopped green pepper
   3 cloves garlic, minced
   1 cup cooked rice
   Salt, to taste
   Freshly ground black pepper, to taste

Sauce:

   3 red bell peppers, seeded and cut in strips
   6 cloves garlic, peeled and split in half
   2 teaspoons olive oil
   1 tablespoon white vinegar
   Water

1. In a food processor, combine $^1/_2$ cups of the cooked peas, bread crumbs, egg, and milk. Process until smooth, stir in remaining split peas, remove from processor, and refrigerate mixture for 1 hour.

2. Meanwhile, prepare the sauce: Preheat oven to 350°F. Place red peppers and oil in a baking dish. Roast for 30 minutes. Add garlic and continue cooking until peppers are soft and garlic is golden, about 30 minutes. Cool slightly and transfer to food processor. Process with vinegar until smooth. Add water through feed tube, 1 teaspoon at a time, as necessary, to desired consistency.

3. Increase oven temperature to 400°F. Heat oil in a large nonstick skillet, over medium flame. Add onion and cook, stirring, until translucent. Add peppers and garlic and cook until peppers are soft, about 5 minutes. Stir in rice and continue cooking for 1 minute. Season with salt and pepper.

4. Stir rice mixture into the cooled pea purée. Combine well.

5. Using a $^1/_4$-cup measure, form patties on a lightly oiled nonstick baking sheet. Bake for 10 minutes, turn, and bake 10 minutes on the other side. Serve with red pepper sauce.

BLACK-EYED PEA FRITTATA

This is an intriguing, slightly spicy yet delicate-tasting dish. The fat-free egg substitutes available now are amazing replacements for the cholesterol-laden egg, and are perfect for frittatas.

Preparation time: 5 minutes
Cooking time: 10 to 15 minutes
Serves 4

1 tablespoon olive oil
2 cups tomato, peeled, diced, and seeded
2 tablespoons chopped jalapeño peppers, seeded
2$^1/_2$ cups cooked black-eyed peas
$^1/_4$ cup chopped fresh cilantro
$^1/_4$ teaspoon freshly ground black pepper
$^1/_4$ teaspoon salt, or to taste
1$^1/_4$ cups fat-free egg substitute

1. Preheat broiler. Heat oil in a 10-inch nonstick skillet over medium-low flame. Add tomatoes and jalapeños and cook, stirring, until peppers are tender, about 2 minutes.

2. Stir in peas, cilantro, salt, and pepper. Add egg substitute and stir until it begins to set. Continue cooking until almost all of the egg is set, lifting the sides of the frittata to allow the raw egg to run underneath.

3. Place skillet under broiler to finish cooking, 4 to 5 minutes. Keep handle of skillet out of oven to avoid melting it or burning yourself. Slide frittata out onto a plate, cut in wedges and serve.

LIGHT-STYLE BAKED BEANS WITH HAM

This is a lovely version of the classic baked beans. The flavor of pork fat that permeates the classic dish is replaced with the slightly smoky flavor of chopped lean ham.

Preparation time: 5 minutes
Cooking time: 2¹/₂ hours
Serves 4 to 5

> 1 tablespoon vegetable oil
> 1 cup chopped onion
> 1 cup chopped carrot
> 2 cloves garlic, minced
> 2 cups canned crushed tomatoes
> 3 cups cooked navy beans
> 1 cup water
> ¹/₃ pound cooked lean ham, diced
> ¹/₄ cup molasses or honey
> 1 tablespoon cider vinegar
> 1 teaspoon mustard powder
> ¹/₄ teaspoon ground cloves

1. Preheat oven to 325°F.

2. Heat oil in a large nonstick skillet or saucepan over medium-low flame. Add onion, carrot, and garlic and cook, stirring occasionally, until onions are tender. Stir in tomatoes, cover, and cook for 5 minutes.

3. Stir beans, water, ham, molasses or honey, vinegar, mustard powder, and cloves into mixture until well combined.

4. Transfer mixture to a baking dish, and bake, covered with foil for 1 hour. Remove foil and continue cooking for $1^1/_2$ hours.

PROVENÇAL LAMB AND TURKEY-SAUSAGE CASSOULET

Here is a simple, light, yet traditionally flavored cassoulet. It makes a perfect home-cooked meal with a distinct French accent.

Preparation time: 15 minutes
Cooking time: 2¹/₂ hours
Serves 7 to 8

1 pound Great Northern beans, soaked
1 onion studded with 4 cloves
¹/₂ teaspoon freshly ground black pepper
2 pounds lamb, cut in ¹/₂-inch cubes
2 tablespoons flour, seasoned with salt and pepper
2 tablespoons olive oil
1 cup chopped onion
¹/₂ cup chopped carrot
¹/₂ cup chopped celery
3 cloves garlic, minced
16 ounces canned plum tomatoes, including liquid
3 cups veal or chicken stock, reduced-sodium chicken broth or water
1¹/₂ teaspoons fresh thyme leaves or ¹/₂ teaspoon dried thyme
1 bay leaf
¹/₂ pound turkey sausage, sliced into ¹/₂-inch rounds

1. In a large saucepan, place beans, clove-studded onion, and pepper in enough water to cover beans, and sim-

mer until tender, about 1 hour. Drain beans and discard onion.

2. Preheat oven to 375°F. Toss the lamb with flour until
well coated. Shake off any excess. Heat oil in a large (4-
quart) Dutch oven, and brown floured lamb on all
sides over medium heat. Remove with a slotted spoon
and set aside.

3. Add onion, carrot, celery, and garlic to pan. Cook, stirring frequently until golden. Return lamb to pan and
add tomatoes, stock, thyme, and bay leaf. Bring mixture to a boil and remove promptly from heat. Add
beans, sausage, and salt and pepper to taste.

4. Place pot in oven, cover and bake for 30 minutes. Uncover and continue cooking until lamb is tender, about
1 hour.

BLACK-EYED PEA, CHICKEN, AND CARROT STEW

This delicate-tasting stew is best served over brown rice or beside a mound of steaming mashed potatoes.

Preparation time: 5 minutes
Cooking time: 10 minutes
Serves 4

> 2 tablespoons olive oil
> $^1/_2$ cup chopped shallots
> 1 pound boneless chicken breast, cut in $^1/_4$-inch by 1$^1/_2$-inch strips
> $^1/_2$ cup flour, seasoned with salt and freshly ground black pepper
> 2 teaspoons dried rosemary leaves
> 1 teaspoon dried tarragon
> 1$^1/_2$ cups sliced carrots
> 3 cups chicken stock or reduced-sodium chicken broth
> 3 cups cooked black-eyed peas
> $^1/_4$ cup water
> 2 teaspoons cornstarch
> 2 teaspoons lemon juice
> Salt, to taste
> Freshly ground black pepper, to taste

1. Heat oil in a large nonstick skillet over medium flame. Add shallots and cook, stirring until tender. Meanwhile, dredge chicken in flour and shake off excess.

2. Add chicken and herbs to oil, and cook, stirring until chicken is golden. Remove chicken from pan and set aside.

3. Add carrots to skillet and cook for 1 minute. Stir in stock and peas. Stir together water, cornstarch, and lemon juice and add it to the stock. Bring mixture to a boil, stirring constantly. Cook until thickened, about 5 minutes.

4. Return chicken to pan to heat through, and season with salt and pepper.

MOROCCAN-STYLE CHICK-PEA AND VEGETABLE COUSCOUS CASSEROLE

The classic flavors of Morocco are baked together in this lovely casserole. Your family will love this vegetarian treat.

Preparation time: 10 minutes
Cooking time: 65 minutes
Serves 5 to 6

> 1 tablespoon vegetable oil
> 1 cup chopped onion
> 1/2 cup diced celery
> 3 cloves garlic, minced
> 1 28-ounce can plum tomatoes, chopped, including liquid
> 2 cups peeled and diced carrots
> 1 1/2 teaspoons ground cumin
> 1/2 teaspoon freshly ground black pepper
> 1-inch piece cinnamon stick
> 1 bay leaf
> 1 cup water
> 1/4 cup chopped parsley
> 4 cups cooked chick-peas
> 3 cups cooked couscous

1. Preheat oven to 350°F.

2. Heat oil in a large (4-quart) saucepan over medium flame. Add onions and celery and cook until translucent. Add carrot, garlic, cumin, pepper, cinnamon stick, and bay leaf and continue cooking for 1 minute, stirring.

3. Stir in tomatoes, water, and parsley. Simmer partially covered until carrot is tender, about 35 minutes. Remove cinnamon stick and bay leaf.

4. Stir chick-peas and couscous into mixture. Transfer to a 3-quart baking dish and bake for 30 minutes.

South American Multi-Bean Chowder

This chowder is based on a soup prepared by the late great chef Felipe Rojas-Lombardi. It is simple and delicious as is, but it is also a lovely base for an even more substantial meal. Feel free to add fish or meat as you desire.

Preparation time: 15 minutes
Cooking time: 1¹/₂ to 2 hours
Serves 6

  2 tablespoons olive oil
  ¹/₂ pound fennel, trimmed and chopped (about 2 cups)
  1¹/₂ pounds leek, trimmed, rinsed, and chopped (about 2 cups)
  2 stalks celery, chopped (¹/₂ cup)
  1 tablespoon grated ginger
  2 cloves garlic, minced
  ³/₄ pound Great Northern beans, soaked
  6 cups water
  ¹/₂ bay leaf
  1 dried chili pepper, seeded
  1¹/₂ cups diced tomatoes
  1¹/₂ cups cooked black-eyed peas
  1¹/₂ cups cooked pinto beans
  2 cups cooked diced potatoes
  ¹/₄ cup chopped parsley or cilantro
  Salt, to taste
  White pepper, to taste

1. Heat oil in a large wide saucepan over medium flame. Add fennel, leeks, and celery. Cook, stirring constantly, until leeks are wilted. Stir in ginger and garlic and continue cooking for 1 minute.

2. Stir in Great Northern beans, water, bay leaf, and chili pepper. Bring mixture to a boil, reduce heat and simmer $1/2$ hour. Remove bay leaf and chili pepper and cool slightly.

3. In batches, transfer mixture to a food processor and process until smooth. Return to saucepan and add black-eyed peas and pinto beans, tomatoes, potatoes, parsley, and salt and pepper. Heat through and serve with lemon wedges.

MAIN DISH SALADS

Chicken, Cannelini Bean, and Broccoli Salad with Creamy Basil Dressing

This salad is a definite crowd pleaser and is perfect with leftover roast chicken.

Preparation time: 5 minutes
Cooking time: None
Serves 4

> 2 cups cooked cannelini beans
> 2 cups cooked chicken, diced
> 2 cups bite-size broccoli florets, steamed to crisp-tender
> 2 cups packed fresh basil leaves
> 1/2 cup packed flat-leaf parsley
> 1/4 cup low-fat or nonfat ricotta cheese
> 3 cloves garlic, cut up
> 2 tablespoons pignoli nuts or chopped walnuts
> 2 tablespoons grated Parmesan cheese
> 1/2 teaspoon freshly ground black pepper
> 1 1/2 tablespoons olive oil
> 2 tablespoons water
> 1/4 teaspoon salt, or to taste

1. Combine beans, chicken, and broccoli in a large bowl. Set aside.

(*Continued on next page*)

2. Place basil, parsley, ricotta, garlic, nuts, cheese, pepper, oil, water, and salt in a food processor and pulse until mixture becomes a smooth paste.

3. Toss basil dressing with beans, chicken, and broccoli until well coated.

SHRIMP AND PASTA SALAD WITH CILANTRO BEAN DRESSING

This salad is very satisfying while remaining light and very low in fat. Beans are puréed to create a thick dressing that replaces the mayonnaise used in many salads.

Preparation time: 15 minutes
Cooking time: None
Serves 4

> 1 pound large shrimp, cooked, peeled, and
>   deveined
> $^1/_2$ pound fusilli, radiatore or other pasta shape,
>   cooked
> $1^1/_2$ cups diced celery
> 2 cups cooked white beans, any variety
> $^1/_3$ cup packed cilantro leaves
> 2 tablespoons lime juice
> 1 clove garlic, minced
> 4 or 5 tablespoons water, as necessary
> 1 tablespoon extra-virgin olive oil
> Salt, to taste

1. Combine shrimp, pasta, and celery in a bowl, and set aside.

2. To prepare dressing: Place beans, cilantro, lime juice, and garlic in a food processor. Process until mixture becomes a smooth paste, adding water, one tablespoon at a time, as necessary. *(Continued on next page)*

3. While the processor is running, slowly add oil, in a thin stream, through the feed tube. Add salt to taste.

4. Toss with shrimp, celery, and pasta and serve on a bed of shredded lettuce.

✎ BLACK BEAN, AVOCADO, AND YELLOW RICE SALAD

This salad was inspired by my regular meal at a local Cuban restaurant: black beans, yellow rice, avocado salad, and a few fiery shots of hot sauce. The combination of beans and rice create a complete protein and thus a healthy meal.

Preparation time: 10 minutes
Cooking time: 20 minutes
Serves 4

2 cups water
1 cup uncooked rice
$^1/_2$ teaspoon powdered turmeric
1 teaspoon vegetable oil
1 teaspoon salt
$2^1/_2$ cups cooked black beans
1 cup diced tomato
$^1/_2$ cup diced roasted red peppers
$^1/_4$ cup chopped sweet white onion
2 tablespoons lemon juice
2 tablespoons olive oil
1 tablespoon white vinegar
Tabasco or other hot sauce, to taste
1 avocado, diced

(*Continued on next page*)

1. In a medium saucepan, heat water to boiling. Add rice, turmeric, oil, and salt. Cover, lower heat and cook until rice is tender, about 20 minutes. Cool slightly.

2. Combine beans, tomato, red peppers, onion, lemon juice, olive oil, vinegar, and Tabasco. Gently toss with rice and avocado.

KIDNEY BEAN, CHICKEN, AND MANGO SALAD

This salad makes a healthy and delicious summer meal. Serve it on a bed of shredded lettuce for a beautiful presentation and a crispy crunch!

Preparation time: 8 minutes
Cooking time: None
Serves 6

2 cups cooked chicken, shredded
3 cups cooked kidney beans
1 large ripe mango, cut in chunks
1 medium tomato, peeled, seeded, and diced
$^3/_4$ cup diced cucumber
$^1/_4$ cup thinly sliced scallion
2 tablespoons chopped walnuts
$^1/_3$ cup orange juice
2 tablespoons olive oil
1 teaspoon white vinegar
$1^1/_2$ teaspoons grated ginger
$^1/_2$ teaspoon salt, or to taste
$^1/_2$ teaspoon freshly ground black pepper

1. Combine chicken, beans, mango, tomato, cucumber, scallion, and walnuts in a nonmetal bowl.

2. In a separate bowl, combine orange juice, olive oil, vinegar, ginger, pepper, and salt. Toss with mango and bean mixture. Serve alone or on a bed of shredded romaine lettuce.

CLASSIC ITALIAN WHITE BEAN AND TUNA SALAD

The Italians soak their onions in water before adding them to salads. This cuts the sharpness of the onions and brings out their sweetness.

Preparation time: 5 minutes, plus ¹/₂ hour to soak onion
Cooking time: None
Serves 4

> ¹/₂ clove garlic, unpeeled
> 3 cups cooked cannelini beans
> 1 cup thinly sliced red onion, soaked in cold water for ¹/₂ hour
> 1 6¹/₂-ounce can water-packed tuna, flaked
> 2 tablespoons finely shredded fresh basil leaves
> 5 teaspoons extra-virgin olive oil
> 1 tablespoon red wine vinegar
> ¹/₄ teaspoon freshly ground black pepper, or to taste
> Salt, to taste
> Radicchio or romaine lettuce leaves

1. Rub a medium-size bowl with the garlic clove. Discard garlic. In the bowl, toss together beans, onion, tuna, basil, oil, vinegar, pepper, and salt.

2. Serve on radicchio or lettuce leaves.

🫘 JAPANESE-FLAVOR ADZUKI BEAN SALAD WITH PORK

The flavors of the Far East come alive in this unusual combination of ingredients. Adzuki beans are available at most health food or Asian specialty stores.

Preparation time: 10 minutes
Cooking time: 5 minutes
Serves 4

   $^1/_2$ pound pork loin, diced in $^1/_4$-inch pieces
   2 teaspoons reduced-sodium soy sauce
   2 teaspoons vegetable oil
   2 cups adzuki beans
   1 cup cooked rice
   1 cup chopped radish
   1 cup chopped cucumber
   1 cup chopped mushrooms
   $^1/_4$ cup thinly sliced scallions
Dressing:
   4 strips of lemon zest, cut in $^1/_2$-inch by 2-inch slivers
   2 tablespoons reduced-sodium soy sauce
   2 tablespoons rice wine vinegar
   2 teaspoons finely chopped ginger
   2 teaspoons honey
   $^1/_2$ teaspoon sesame oil

1. Combine pork and 2 teaspoons soy sauce. Heat oil in a large nonstick skillet over medium flame. Add pork and cook until just cooked through.

(*Continued on next page*)

2. In a large bowl, combine pork, beans, rice, radish, cucumber, mushrooms, and scallions, and set aside.

3. In a separate bowl, whisk together lemon zest, soy sauce, vinegar, ginger, honey, and sesame oil. Toss with bean mixture and serve.

PASTAS

RED PEPPER AND TOMATO BEAN SAUCE

This is a wonderful rich tomato and red pepper sauce. It is as thick and hearty as a meat sauce, and rich in low-fat vegetable protein. Serve it over a large-shape pasta such as rigatoni.

Preparation time: 10 minutes
Cooking time: 35 minutes
Serves 4 to 5

2 teaspoons olive oil
1 cup chopped onion
4 cloves garlic, minced
1¹/₂ cups chopped red bell pepper
2 cups canned plum tomatoes
2 cups cooked pinto beans
2 cups beef stock, reduced-sodium beef broth, or water
¹/₂ teaspoon dried thyme
¹/₂ teaspoon crushed red pepper
¹/₄ teaspoon marjoram
1 bay leaf
1 tablespoon vinegar
Salt, to taste
Freshly ground black pepper, to taste

1. Heat oil in a large (4-quart) heavy-bottom saucepan over medium flame. Add onion and garlic and cook, stirring until onion is tender, about 3 minutes. Add red

bell pepper and continue cooking until the pepper is tender, another 5 minutes.

2. Add tomatoes, beans, stock, thyme, red pepper, marjoram, and bay leaf. Bring mixture to a boil, reduce heat and simmer, stirring occasionally, for 30 minutes. Remove bay leaf and cool slightly.

3. Transfer $2/3$ of the mixture to a food processor and process until chunky-smooth. Return purée to pot and add vinegar, salt, and pepper. Bring to a boil and serve over rigatoni.

PASTA WITH WHITE BEANS AND CLAM SAUCE

Once again, the bean triumphs as the ultimate sauce thickener. The sauce is creamy and rich, yet very light and low in fat compared to flour- or cream-thickened sauces of the past.

Preparation time: 5 minutes
Cooking time: 20 minutes
Serves 4 to 6

> **1 pound linguini, shells, or other pasta shape**
> **1 tablespoon olive oil**
> **4 cloves garlic, minced**
> **2 8-ounce bottles clam juice**
> **3 cups cooked small white beans**
> **1/2 teaspoon dried thyme leaves**
> **2 6 1/2-ounce cans minced clams, including juice**
> **1/4 cup chopped parsley**
> **Salt, to taste**
> **Freshly ground black pepper, to taste**

1. Cook pasta according to package directions. Drain.

2. Heat oil in a large nonstick skillet over medium-low flame. Add garlic and cook, stirring, until tender. Stir in clam juice and juice from the minced clams, then beans and thyme. Simmer for 5 minutes. Cool slightly.

(*Continued on next page*)

3. Transfer the mixture to a food processor and process until smooth.

4. Return mixture to skillet. Add clams, parsley, salt, and pepper and heat through. Toss with cooked pasta and serve.

PASTA AND VEGETABLES WITH CHEESY WHITE BEAN SAUCE

Puréed beans make a lovely rich sauce without the fat of the butter that we're used to. Try serving this dish to the children when you want to sneak them some bean protein.

Preparation time: 15 minutes
Cooking time: 10 minutes, plus pasta cooking time
Serves 4

> 1 pound penne, or other large pasta shape
> 2 cups cooked white beans
> ³/₄ cup low-fat milk
> 2 teaspoons fresh thyme leaves or ¹/₂ teaspoon dried thyme
> 1 cup shredded reduced-fat cheddar cheese
> 2 tablespoons grated Parmesan cheese
> ¹/₂ teaspoon freshly ground black pepper, or to taste
> ¹/₄ teaspoon grated nutmeg
> Salt, to taste
> 2 cups broccoli florets, cut into 1-inch pieces, steamed to crisp-tender
> 2 cups cauliflower florets, cut into 1-inch pieces, steamed to crisp-tender
> 1¹/₂ cups quartered cherry tomatoes
> ¹/₂ cup cooked peas
> 2 tablespoons chopped fresh basil leaves

(*Continued on next page*)

1. Cook pasta according to package directions. Drain.

2. Place beans and milk in a food processor, and process until very smooth.

3. Transfer mixture to a saucepan and heat over medium-low, until just simmering. Stir in cheeses, nutmeg, pepper, and salt. Stir until melted.

4. Toss cheese sauce with pasta, broccoli, cauliflower, tomatoes, peas, and basil and serve.

SPINACH AND CHICK-PEA SHELLS

This is a great homestyle pasta dish, perfect for a hearty meal with friends or family.

Preparation time: 5 minutes
Cooking time: 15 minutes
Serves 4 to 5

> 1 pound pasta shells
> ³/₄ cup chopped onion
> 1 tablespoon olive oil
> 1¹/₂ cup finely diced red bell pepper
> 2 cups cooked chick-peas
> 3 tablespoons chopped fresh dill
> 1 cup water
> ¹/₂ cup tomato paste (1 small can)
> ¹/₂ teaspoon freshly ground black pepper, or to taste
> Salt, to taste
> 3¹/₂ cups chopped spinach leaves
> 2 tablespoons pignoli (pine) nuts

1. Cook pasta shells until tender, drain and set aside.

2. In a large nonstick skillet, cook onion in oil over medium heat a few minutes, until tender. Add red pepper and continue cooking until peppers are tender. Add chick-peas and dill and toss to coat.

(Continued on next page)

3. Stir in the water, tomato paste, pepper, and salt. Cover and simmer for 5 minutes.

4. Add spinach to chick-peas and cook until just wilted. Toss pasta shells with sauce and pignoli nuts. Serve promptly.

 # MEXICAN LASAGNE

Think of the surprise at the first bite of this lasagne when everyone tastes the unconventional fillings. And then think of the smiles, bravos, and requests for it in the future.

Preparation time: 30 minutes
Cooking time: 45 to 55 minutes
Serves 6

¹/₂ pound lasagne noodles
2 tablespoons olive oil
2 medium onions, thinly sliced
2 red peppers, cored and cut in ¹/₈-inch-wide strips
2 green peppers, cored and cut in ¹/₈-inch-wide strips
2 medium zucchini, sliced ¹/₈-inch thick
2 yellow squash, sliced ¹/₈-inch thick
Salt, to taste
Freshly ground black pepper, to taste
1 tablespoon vegetable oil
3 cups cooked kidney, pinto, or black beans
3 cloves garlic, minced
2 teaspoons chili powder
1 teaspoon ground cumin
¹/₈ teaspoon cayenne pepper
¹/₂ cup water
2¹/₂ cups homemade or canned tomato sauce
1 cup shredded reduced-fat cheddar cheese

1. Preheat oven to 300°F.

(*Continued on next page*)

2. Cook lasagne noodles in plenty of water, until just tender. Drain and place in cold water until needed.

3. Heat 2 tablespoons olive oil in a large nonstick skillet over medium flame. Add onion and cook, stirring until soft. Add peppers, zucchini, and squash and cook until tender, about 20 minutes. Season with salt and pepper to taste.

4. Meanwhile, heat 1 tablespoon vegetable oil in a large nonstick skillet over medium-low flame. Add garlic, chili powder, cumin, and cayenne pepper and cook for 1 minute. Stir in beans, add water, cover, and cook for 3 minutes. Cool slightly.

5. Place cooled bean mixture in a food processor. Process until smooth and spreadable (add a little water, if necessary).

6. In a 9-inch by 13-inch lasagne pan, spread $1/2$ cup tomato sauce, and layer pasta sheets, $1/2$ of the bean mixture, then $1/2$ cup sauce, $1/2$ of the vegetable mixture, and $1/3$ cup cheese; repeat. Spread top with remaining sauce and sprinkle with remaining cheese.

7. Bake until cheese is melted and sauce is bubbly, about 45 minutes. Allow lasagne to sit for 10 minutes before cutting.

SALADS

 SOUTHWESTERN BLACK BEAN SALAD

This is a flavorful and colorful salad. But feel free to break from the Southwest theme by eating it, as I do, stuffed in a pita with shredded romaine lettuce.

Preparation time: 5 minutes
Cooking time: None
Serves 4

1 tablespoon ground cumin
2 tablespoons lime juice
1 tablespoon extra-virgin olive or vegetable oil
1 teaspoon white vinegar
$^1/_4$ teaspoon salt
$1^1/_2$ cups cooked black beans
$^1/_2$ cup finely diced carrot
$^1/_2$ cup cooked corn kernels
3 tablespoons chopped cilantro
2 tablespoons chopped red onion

1. Heat cumin in a small skillet over a low flame just until fragrant, about 1 minute.

2. Whisk together cumin, lime juice, oil, and salt.

3. Combine beans, carrot, corn, cilantro, and onion. Toss with dressing.

LEMONY WHITE BEAN SALAD

I could eat this salad every day! Make a large batch and reserve leftovers; each day that it stays in the refrigerator, it gets better tasting. You can use canned beans, but I prefer this method because hot beans absorb the flavors much better.

Preparation time: 5 minutes, plus cooling and marination time.
Cooking time: About 2 hours
Serves 5 to 6

> 2 cups small white beans, soaked
> 1 clove garlic
> 1 teaspoon salt
> 1 cup thinly sliced scallions
> 1/4 cup lemon juice
> 3 tablespoons extra-virgin olive oil
> 1 tablespoon white vinegar
> 1/4 cup chopped fresh parsley
> 1 tablespoon chopped dill
> 1 teaspoon chopped fresh mint

1. In a medium saucepan, place beans in enough water to cover and cook until tender but not broken, about 2 hours. Drain well and transfer to a bowl.

2. Chop garlic with salt and add it to hot beans along with scallions, lemon juice, oil, and vinegar. Toss well and set aside until cool.

3. Add chopped herbs and refrigerate salad for at least 1 hour before serving.

HERBED FRENCH LENTIL SALAD

This is a classic, delicious salad—flecked with herbs. Be sure not to overcook the lentils—they should remain whole!

Preparation time: 5 minutes, plus cooling time
Cooking time: 20 to 30 minutes
Serves 4

> 1 cup lentils
> 1 bay leaf
> 1/2 cup finely diced red bell pepper
> 1/2 cup finely diced green bell pepper
> 1/2 cup chopped sweet white onion
> 2 tablespoons chopped parsley
> 2 tablespoons extra-virgin olive oil
> 1 tablespoon chopped fresh sage
> 1 tablespoon white wine vinegar
> Salt, to taste
> Freshly ground pepper, to taste

1. In a medium saucepan, place lentils with bay leaf in plenty of boiling water, and cook until just tender, 20 to 30 minutes. Drain well and remove bay leaf.

2. Toss hot lentils with peppers, onions, parsley, oil, sage, vinegar, salt, and pepper. Cool to room temperature and serve.

MARINATED THREE-BEAN SALAD

Three beautiful colors and crisp flavors make this salad a simple treat. Marinate it overnight for a really wonderful taste.

Preparation time: 5 minutes
Cooking time: 3 minutes
Serves 4

- $^1/_2$ **pound fresh green beans, trimmed and cut into 1-inch lengths**
- $^1/_4$ **cup red wine vinegar**
- **4 teaspoons extra-virgin olive oil**
- $^1/_4$ **cup shredded fresh basil leaves**
- $^1/_4$ **teaspoon freshly ground black pepper**
- **1 teaspoon sugar**
- **1$^1/_2$ cups red bell pepper cut into 1-inch by $^1/_4$-inch strips**
- **1 cup cooked red kidney beans**
- **1 cup cooked chick-peas**

1. Bring a large pot of water to the boil. Cook green beans just until crisp-tender, about 3 minutes. Drain.

2. Whisk together vinegar, oil, basil, pepper, and sugar.

3. Place hot green beans and red pepper strips in a shallow dish. Add cooked beans, pour marinade over, and gently toss. Cover and marinate for at least one hour. Serve chilled.

PINTO BEAN SALAD WITH HAM

This is a lovely light bean salad which packs a very robust flavor. Try serving it hot as a side dish by heating it quickly in a nonstick skillet.

Preparation time: 8 minutes
Cooking time: None
Serves 4

> 3 cups pinto beans
> 1¹/₂ cups diced celery
> ¹/₂ cup diced cooked ham
> 2 tablespoons crumbled blue cheese (optional)
> 3 tablespoons chopped fresh dill
> 3 tablespoons chopped fresh parsley
> 2 tablespoons red wine vinegar
> 1 tablespoon extra-virgin olive oil
> 2 cloves garlic, minced
> 1 teaspoon chopped fresh sage or ¹/₂ teaspoon dried sage (if using dry, chop with parsley)
> ¹/₄ teaspoon freshly ground black pepper

1. In a bowl combine beans, celery, ham, and cheese if desired. Set aside.

2. In a separate bowl, whisk together dill, parsley, vinegar, oil, garlic, sage, and pepper. Toss with bean mixture and serve.

₷ ROMAN KIDNEY BEAN SALAD

This is a version of an Italian poor-man's salad. Originally made with day-old bread, this salad has the robust flavors of a feast.

Preparation time: 10 minutes, plus ¹/₂ hour marination time
Cooking time: None
Serves 4

4 anchovy filets
1 tablespoon capers, drained
1 clove garlic, minced
Pinch salt
1 tablespoon olive oil
2 teaspoons red wine vinegar
1 teaspoon lemon juice
2 cups cooked kidney beans
1 cup tomato diced
1 cup diced celery
¹/₃ cup chopped red onion

1. Chop anchovies and capers with garlic and salt until mixture is almost smooth. Transfer paste to a small bowl and whisk it together with oil, vinegar, and lemon juice.

2. Combine kidney beans, tomato, celery, and onion in a large nonmetal bowl. Toss with anchovy mixture and refrigerate for 30 minutes.

BARLEY BEAN SALAD

Here is a lovely, refreshing salad which is hearty enough for a meal. Served on a bed of mixed greens, it makes a colorful, festive dish.

Preparation time: 5 minutes
Cooking time: None
Serves 6

3 cups cooked black beans
2 cups cooked barley
1¹/₂ cups cooked yellow corn
1 cup diced red bell pepper
4 scallions, thinly sliced
3 tablespoons extra-virgin olive oil
3 tablespoons balsamic or red wine vinegar
2 tablespoons lime juice
Salt, to taste
Freshly ground black pepper, to taste

1. In a large nonmetal bowl, combine black beans, barley, corn, red pepper, and scallion.

2. In a separate bowl, whisk together oil, vinegar, lime juice, salt, and pepper. Toss with bean mixture.

WHITE BEAN AND WATERCRESS SALAD WITH TOMATO DRESSING

By vigorously stirring the tomatoes with the other dressing ingredients they give up their juice. This becomes the base of the dressing. The other ingredients round out the Italian flavor of the dish.

Preparation time: 5 minutes
Cooking time: None
Serves 4

2 cups cooked small white beans
1 cup torn watercress or arugula leaves
2 cups slivered cherry tomatoes
6 olives, pitted and slivered
2 tablespoons shredded basil leaves
1 tablespoon extra-virgin olive oil
2 teaspoons red wine vinegar
1 clove garlic, minced
$^1/_4$ teaspoon freshly ground black pepper
1 tablespoon grated Parmesan cheese

1. In a large bowl, mix together the beans and watercress or arugula leaves. Set aside.

2. In a separate bowl, combine tomatoes, olives, basil, olive oil, vinegar, garlic, and pepper. Stir vigorously until well combined. Toss with beans, watercress, and Parmesan.

SUCCOTASH VINAIGRETTE

Lima beans grow up! This is nothing like the succotash you remember. It has a lovely sophisticated flavor that you and your family will love.

Preparation time: 5 minutes
Cooking time: 5 to 6 minutes
Serves 4

> 1 cup frozen corn kernels
> 1 teaspoon dijon mustard
> 1¹/₂ tablespoons balsamic or good red wine vinegar
> 1 tablespoon extra-virgin olive oil
> 2 cups cooked dried lima beans
> ¹/₄ cup finely diced red onion
> ¹/₄ cup diced red bell pepper
> Salt, to taste
> Freshly ground black pepper, to taste

1. Cook corn until tender, about 5 or 6 minutes.

2. Meanwhile, whisk together the mustard and vinegar. Slowly add oil to mixture while whisking. Toss with lima beans, corn, onion, and red pepper. Sprinkle with salt and pepper. Cool before serving.

BLACK-EYED PEA SALAD WITH LEMON AND MINT

This is such a simple salad, but it is so fresh and delicious. Serve it in the summer with chicken fresh off the grill, or at an all-salad luncheon.

Preparation time: 5 minutes
Cooking time: None
Serves 4

3 cups cooked black-eyed peas
2 cups diced cucumber
1 cup diced seeded tomato
6 tablespoons chopped fresh mint
$^1/_4$ cup thinly sliced scallions
2 tablespoons lemon juice
4 teaspoons extra-virgin olive oil
Salt, to taste

1. In a large nonmetal bowl, combine peas, cucumber, tomato, mint, and scallions.

2. Whisk together oil, lemon juice, and salt. Toss with pea mixture. Serve cool.

LENTIL AND ORANGE SALAD

This combination of lentils and orange is a brilliant contrast. The slightly nutty flavor of the lentils complement the sweet and sour of the orange—an exotic treat!

Preparation time: 5 minutes
Cooking time: None
Serves 4 to 5

4 cups cooked lentils
2 large oranges, sectioned, peel and pith removed
¹/₂ cup chopped red onion
¹/₄ cup thinly shredded basil leaves
2 tablespoons apple cider vinegar
4 teaspoons extra-virgin olive oil
¹/₄ teaspoon salt, or to taste

1. In a large nonmetal bowl, combine lentils, orange, onion, and basil.

2. Whisk together vinegar, oil, and salt. Toss with lentil and orange mixture. Serve at room temperature.

FRUITED WILD RICE AND BEAN SALAD

Everyone loves this healthy salad—crunchy and sweet—it's a must for the buffet table.

Preparation time: 10 minutes, plus cooling time
Cooking time: 45 minutes
Serves 6

1 cup wild rice
5 cups chicken stock or reduced-sodium chicken
   broth
3 cups cooked small red beans
3/4 cup golden raisins
1/2 cup broken pecans
1/3 cup thinly sliced scallions
1/4 cup chopped fresh mint
1 tablespoon grated orange zest
2 cans mandarin orange sections, including liquid
2 tablespoons extra-virgin olive oil
Salt, to taste
Freshly ground black pepper, to taste
1 cup grapes, halved

1. In a large saucepan, bring stock to a boil. Stir in wild rice, reduce heat and simmer, uncovered, until tender, about 45 minutes. Drain well and transfer to a large bowl.

(Continued on next page)

2. Add beans, raisins, nuts, scallion, mint, orange zest, mandarin oranges, oil, pepper, and salt. Toss well. Cover and let salad cool to room temperature.

3. Add grapes and serve at room temperature or refrigerate and serve cool.

CRUNCHY CURRIED YELLOW SPLIT PEA, BROWN RICE, AND APPLE SALAD

Split peas can be a different and delicious addition to your salad repertoire. Cook them until they are just tender. If cooked too long they will get mushy.

Preparation time: 10 minutes
Cooking time: 1 minute
Serves 5 to 6

2 cups yellow split peas, cooked until just tender
1¹/₂ cups cooked brown rice
1 cup chopped red delicious apple
1 cup chopped celery
¹/₂ cup chopped onion
¹/₂ cup chopped carrot
¹/₃ cup diced red bell pepper
¹/₄ cup golden raisins
1¹/₂ teaspoons curry powder
Pinch cinnamon
¹/₃ cup low-fat yogurt
3 tablespoons reduced-fat mayonnaise
2 teaspoons cider vinegar

1. In a large bowl, combine peas, rice, apple, celery, onion, carrots, pepper, and raisins and set aside.

2. In a small skillet, heat curry powder and cinnamon over very low flame until just fragrant, about 1 minute. Combine yogurt, mayonnaise, and vinegar. Stir in curry mixture and toss with yellow pea and rice mixture. Serve cool.

CHICK-PEA AND MACARONI SALAD

This is a healthy twist on the classic macaroni salad. The usual mayonnaise is replaced by light mayonnaise and low-fat yogurt and the nutrition is boosted with chick-peas.

Preparation time: 10 minutes
Cooking time: None
Serves 6

> 3 cups cooked chick-peas
> 3 cups cooked macaroni
> $^1/_2$ cup chopped celery
> $^1/_4$ cup low-fat yogurt
> $^1/_4$ cup chopped red pepper
> $^1/_4$ cup chopped green pepper
> 3 tablespoons chopped onion
> 2 tablespoons light mayonnaise
> 1 tablespoon red wine vinegar
> Freshly ground black pepper, to taste

1. In a large bowl, combine chick-peas, macaroni, celery, yogurt, peppers, onion, mayonnaise, vinegar, and pepper. Toss well and serve.

SIDE DISHES

 **REFRIED BEANS**

Refried beans is a traditional Mexican dish; but it is also delicious with other flavors. Here I have given a choice between the traditional Mexican and Indian flavorings.

Preparation time: 2 minutes
Cooking time: 12 to 15 minutes
Serves 5 to 6

1¹/₂ tablespoons vegetable oil
2 cups chopped onion
3 cloves garlic, minced
2 teaspoons curry *or* chili powder
4 cups cooked pinto beans
Water
2 tablespoons thinly sliced chives
Salt, to taste

1. Heat oil in a large nonstick skillet over medium-low flame. Add onion, garlic, and curry or chili powder. Cook, stirring until onion is tender.

2. Add 1 tablespoon water and beans, ¹/₄ cup at a time, mashing them into onion. Mixture should be fairly dry, but if it becomes too dry, mix in more water, 1 tablespoon at a time, until fully mashed.

3. Add chives and salt and mix thoroughly. Serve promptly.

LIGHT-STYLE CUBAN BLACK BEANS

Serve this classic dish with white, yellow, or brown rice. A large plate of beans and rice with a salad makes a hearty, healthful, and inexpensive meal. Keep a bottle of hot sauce on hand, for authenticity and a bit of zing.

Preparation time: 5 minutes
Cooking time: 1¹/₂ hours
Serves 4

> ¹/₂ **pound soaked black beans**
> **3 cups water**
> **1¹/₂ cups chopped onion**
> **1 cup chopped green pepper**
> ¹/₄ **cup packed fresh cilantro leaves**
> ¹/₂ **teaspoon oregano**
> **1 bay leaf**
> **2 tablespoons olive oil**
> **1 clove garlic, minced**
> ¹/₂ **cup diced red pepper**
> **2 tablespoons vinegar**
> **Pinch sugar**
> **Salt, to taste**

1. In a 3-quart saucepan, combine beans, water, ³/₄ cup of onion, ¹/₂ cup of green pepper, cilantro, oregano, and bay leaf. Bring to a boil, reduce heat immediately, and simmer until beans are very tender, about 1¹/₂ hours. There should be some liquid left. If you see that too

much liquid is evaporating during cooking, add a little
more water.

2. Meanwhile, heat oil in a nonstick skillet over medium
flame, add garlic, red peppers, remaining green peppers, and remaining onion. Cook, stirring, until vegetables are tender.

3. Stir vegetables into cooked beans, along with vinegar,
sugar, and salt. Mash a few beans against side of pan, to
thicken mixture. Heat to boiling and serve over rice.

MASHED SPLIT PEAS AND POTATOES

This is a wonderful, fresh and nutritious alternative to plain mashed potatoes. Use your imagination to experiment with other additions.

Preparation time: 10 minutes
Cooking time: 30 to 35 minutes
Serves 6

2 tablespoons olive oil
1½ cups chopped onion
2 cloves garlic, minced
3 cups peeled, cubed potatoes
1½ cups yellow split peas
2 cups chicken broth or reduced-sodium chicken broth
2½ cups water
½ teaspoon ground cumin
1 cup diced tomatoes
2 tablespoons chopped olives
2 tablespoons lemon juice
2 teaspoons fresh thyme leaves
Salt, to taste

1. Heat olive oil in a large saucepan over medium-high flame. Add onions and garlic and cook until tender. Stir in potatoes and continue cooking until onions just begin to turn golden.

2. Stir in peas, broth, water, and cumin. Bring to a boil, lower heat, and simmer, partially covered, until peas are tender, 30 to 35 minutes. Drain.

3. Transfer drained mixture to a large bowl and mash with a potato masher. When mixture is smooth, stir in tomatoes, olives, lemon juice, thyme, and salt.

LENTILS WITH SPINACH AND GINGER

Lentils aren't just for soup anymore! Try this lovely sautéed lentil dish for a tasty change at dinner.

Preparation time: 5 minutes
Cooking time: 15 minutes
Serves 4

> **2 teaspoons olive oil**
> **1/2 cup chopped onion**
> **2 cloves garlic**
> **1/2 cup finely diced red bell pepper**
> **1/2 cup finely diced carrot**
> **1 tablespoon grated ginger**
> **2 cups cooked lentils**
> **1 10-ounce package frozen chopped spinach,**
>   **defrosted and drained**
> **1 cup water**
> **1 teaspoon reduced-sodium soy sauce**

1. Heat oil in a large nonstick skillet over medium flame. Add onion and garlic and cook, stirring, until onion is transluscent. Add red pepper, carrot, and ginger and continue cooking until onion is golden.

2. Stir in lentils, spinach, and water, cover and simmer for 10 minutes. Sprinkle with soy sauce and serve.

Lima Beans with Lemon and Poppy Seeds

The flavors of this lima bean dish are classic and simple. Try serving them at an elegant dinner. They look beautiful on the plate.

Preparation time: 5 minutes
Cooking time: 10 to 12 minutes
Serves 4

1 tablespoon olive oil
1 clove garlic, minced
3 cups cooked dried lima beans
1¹/₂ cups chicken stock, reduced-sodium chicken
   broth or water
¹/₄ cup, plus 2 tablespoons lemon juice
1 teaspoon grated lemon zest
1 teaspoon cornstarch
¹/₂ cup scallions
2 tablespoons poppy seeds

1. Heat oil in a large nonstick skillet over medium-low flame. Add garlic and cook, stirring, for 1 minute. Add beans, 1 cup stock, ¹/₄ cup lemon juice, and lemon zest. Simmer until flavors are combined, 6 to 7 minutes.

2. Meanwhile, whisk remaining stock and lemon juice with cornstarch. Stir cornstarch mixture into beans. Bring it to a boil and cook, stirring constantly, until sauce has thickened. Toss limas with scallions and poppy seeds and serve promptly.

GREEK-STYLE BRAISED CHICK-PEAS

This is a lovely dish that my Greek-American friend, Rhea, makes for me as her grandmother did, and her mother still does, for her. Served with rice, it can be a simple meal.

Preparation time: 5 minutes
Cooking time: 30 minutes
Serves 6

1 tablespoon olive oil
2 cups chopped onion
3 cloves garlic, minced
1 14-ounce can plum tomatoes, including liquid
1 cup water
4 cups cooked chick-peas
$^1/_3$ cup chopped parsley
$^1/_4$ cup chopped fresh mint
3 tablespoons lemon juice
Salt, to taste
$^1/_2$ teaspoon freshly ground black pepper

1. Heat oil in a large saucepan over medium-low flame. Add onion and garlic and cook, stirring, until just tender. Stir in tomatoes and water and continue cooking for 1 minute.

2. Add chick-peas, parsley, and mint. Bring mixture to a boil, reduce heat, and gently simmer for 20 minutes. Add lemon juice, salt, and pepper and cook for 5 minutes.

Garlicky White Beans and Escarole

This dish is for garlic lovers only! But don't be alarmed; the garlic is well mellowed by the beans and a bit of cooking.

Preparation time: 10 minutes
Cooking time: 15 minutes
Serves 6

> 1 tablespoon olive oil
> 8 cloves garlic, minced
> 3 cups cooked Great Northern beans
> 1 cup diced plum tomato
> 1 cup water
> 1 tablespoon white vinegar
> 4 cups torn escarole leaves
> Salt, to taste
> Freshly ground black pepper, to taste

1. Heat oil in a large nonstick skillet over medium-low flame. Add garlic and cook, stirring, until tender.

2. Add beans and tomato and stir to coat. Add water and vinegar, cover, and cook for 5 minutes.

3. Stir in escarole, add salt and pepper, cover, and cook, stirring occasionally until escarole is tender but still bright green, 5 to 6 minutes.

CANNELINI MARGHERITA

Cannelini beans are lovely combined with the flavors of a classic Italian pizza topping—tomatoes, basil, and cheese. The children will love this dish because the flavors are familiar to them. Add little bits of pepperoni or sausage to continue the theme.

Preparation time: 3 minutes
Cooking time: 5 minutes
Serves 4

> 2 teaspoons olive oil
> 1 clove garlic, minced
> 1 cup chopped canned plum tomatoes, without liquid
> 2 cups cooked cannelini beans, rinse and drain if
>   canned
> 2 tablespoons chopped fresh basil
> 2 tablespoons grated Parmesan

1. Heat oil in a large nonstick saucepan over medium-low flame. Add garlic and cook, stirring, until tender.

2. Stir in tomatoes and beans. Simmer for 3 minutes, stirring occasionally.

3. Sprinkle with basil and Parmesan, stir well and serve.

🫘 VEGETABLE BEAN CASSEROLE PARMESAN

This lovely bean casserole has the robust flavor of Parmesan cheese and a beautiful sauce made from natural vegetable juices.

Preparation time: 10 minutes
Cooking time: 55 minutes
Serves 4 to 6

2 red bell peppers, slivered
2 cups diced tomatoes
2 cups onion, slivered
1 cup diagonally sliced celery
4 cloves garlic, slivered
1 teaspoon fresh thyme leaves
$^1/_2$ teaspoon dried oregano
1 tablespoon olive oil
3 cups cooked kidney beans
2 cups water
3 tablespoons grated Parmesan cheese
Freshly ground black pepper, to taste

1. Preheat oven to 375°F.

2. Toss peppers, tomato, onion, celery, garlic, thyme, and oregano with olive oil. Place in oven and roast for 35 minutes, tossing occasionally.

3. Stir in beans and water and return to oven for 20 minutes. Toss with cheese and pepper.

SMOTHERED BEANS WITH SAUSAGE AND PEPPERS

This slow-cooked bean dish has a rich smoky taste. The sausage has a lot of flavor, but since so little is used, the fat content of the dish is still quite low.

Preparation time: 5 minutes
Cooking time: 45 to 50 minutes
Serves 4 to 5

2 ounces sausage meat, removed from casing
2 cups pinto beans
1 cup diced red bell pepper
1 cup diced green bell pepper
1 cup chopped onion
³/₄ cup chicken stock or reduced-sodium chicken broth
3 cloves garlic, minced
Salt, to taste
Freshly ground black pepper, to taste

1. Cook sausage in a large nonstick skillet over medium heat, breaking it up as it is stirred. When sausage is cooked, remove from pan, wipe pan clean, and return sausage to pan.

2. Add beans, peppers, onion, stock, and garlic, cover and cook over medium heat for 40 minutes, stirring occasionally. Add salt and pepper, to taste.

ORANGY SWEET POTATO WITH RED AND WHITE KIDNEY BEANS

This is a wonderful homey dish perfect with chicken, turkey or game. Don't worry about overcooking the beans; the acid in the orange juice will keep them from getting too soft.

Preparation time: 5 minutes
Cooking time: 75 to 90 minutes
Serves 4 to 5

2 cups cubed (^{1}/$_2$-inch) peeled sweet potatoes
1 cup cooked red kidney beans
1 cup cooked white kidney beans
1^1/$_2$ cups orange juice
2 teaspoons olive oil
^{3}/$_4$ teaspoon dried sage
1 clove garlic, minced
^{1}/$_2$ teaspoon salt
Pinch ground cloves

1. Preheat oven to 375°F. Place potatoes in a 1-quart casserole. Top with beans.

2. Stir together orange juice, olive oil, sage, garlic, salt, and cloves. Pour juice mixture over sweet potato and beans. Place in oven and cook, stirring two or three times, until potatoes are tender, 75 to 90 minutes. Allow dish to cool for 5 minutes before serving.

CANNELINI BEANS AND POTATOES GREMOLATA

Gremolata is the brilliant combination of parsley, lemon zest, garlic, and pepper. Sprinkled over potatoes and beans it makes a lovely dish.

Preparation time: 5 minutes
Cooking time: 20 to 25 minutes
Serves 4

> 1 pound small red new potatoes
> 2 cups cooked cannelini beans
> 2 tablespoons extra-virgin olive oil
> $^1/_3$ cup chopped parsley
> 3 cloves garlic, minced
> 1 tablespoon grated lemon zest
> 1 teaspoon salt
> $^3/_4$ teaspoon freshly ground black pepper

1. Boil potatoes in plenty of water until tender, 20 to 25 minutes. Drain potatoes well and slice $^1/_4$-inch thick. Heat beans until just warm. Toss warm potatoes and beans with olive oil.

2. To prepare the gremolata: Combine parsley, garlic, lemon zest, salt, and pepper and chop all together until very fine. Sprinkle the gremolata over warm potatoes and beans.

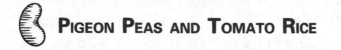

PIGEON PEAS AND TOMATO RICE

This is a very flavorful dish cooked in just enough bacon to give a slightly smoky aroma and little enough oil to keep it light. Serve it as a side dish, but remember, it has all the nutrition to be served as a meal by itself.

Preparation time: 5 minutes
Cooking time: 35 to 40 minutes
Serves 6

> 2 strips bacon, chopped
> 1 cup chopped onion
> 2 cloves garlic, minced
> 1 cup rice
> $^1/_2$ pound pigeon peas, cooked (4 to 5 cups)
> 1 14-ounce can plum tomatoes, juice reserved
> $1^3/_4$ to 2 cups chicken stock or reduced-sodium
>   chicken broth
> $^1/_2$ teaspoon crushed hot red pepper flakes
> $^1/_4$ teaspoon salt
> Pinch allspice
> 1 bay leaf

1. Slowly cook bacon in a large wide saucepan until crisp. Pour off excess fat but do not wipe pan. Add onion and garlic to pan and cook over medium heat, stirring, until tender.

2. Stir rice into onion and bacon mixture, just to coat. Add peas, tomatoes, reserved tomato juice plus stock

to make $2^1/_4$ cups, hot pepper flakes, salt, allspice, and bay leaf.

3. Heat mixture to boiling. Cover, reduce heat, and simmer until liquid is absorbed, about 30 minutes. Remove bay leaf. Serve hot.

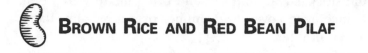 BROWN RICE AND RED BEAN PILAF

This pilaf has a brilliant sweetness and the intriguing flavors of the Middle East. Don't forget, the combination of rice and beans makes a complete protein and children will enjoy this healthful side dish, even if they don't eat their main course.

Preparation time: 5 minutes
Cooking time: 45 to 50 minutes
Serves 4 to 5

  1 tablespoon vegetable oil
  1 cup chopped onion
  1 tablespoon chopped orange zest
  1-inch cinnamon stick
  $^1/_2$ teaspoon ground cumin
  1 cup long grain brown rice
  2 tablespoons currants
  $2^1/_2$ cups chicken stock, reduced-sodium chicken
     broth or water
  $^1/_2$ teaspoon sugar
  $^1/_2$ teaspoon salt
  2 cups cooked red beans

1. Heat oil in a large (4-quart) wide saucepan over medium flame. Add onions and cook, stirring, until tender. Stir in orange zest, cinnamon stick, and cumin, then rice and currants. Stir to coat.

(*Continued on next page*)

2. Add stock, sugar, and salt and bring mixture to a boil. Reduce heat, cover, and simmer over a very low flame for 35 minutes.

3. Stir beans into rice and continue cooking until rice is tender, about 10 minutes. If there is liquid in the mixture, uncover pot, increase heat, and stir gently until it has evaporated.

 HERBED HOPPIN' JOHN

This is an updated verson of the classic Hoppin' John. Its flavors are bright and fresh and it is very pretty on the plate.

Preparation time: 5 minutes
Cooking time: 5 minutes
Serves 6

4 teaspoons olive oil
1 cup chopped onion
1 cup diced tomato
3 cups cooked black-eyed peas
3 cups cooked rice
3 tablespoons chopped parsley
1 tablespoon chopped basil leaves
1 tablespoon chopped fresh rosemary, thyme leaves
   or a combination
1/2 teaspoon salt, or to taste
Freshly ground black pepper, to taste

1. Heat oil in a large nonstick skillet over medium flame. Add onion and cook, stirring, until translucent. Add tomato and cook for 1 minute more.

2. Stir in peas, rice, parsley, basil, and rosemary or thyme and continue cooking, tossing gently, for 3 minutes. Season with salt and pepper.

SWEETS

Raspberry Almond Bean Pie

Who would believe that puréed beans would make such a fabulous filling for a pie? Creamy and custardy, it's perfectly offset by the slight tartness of the raspberries.

Preparation time: 5 minutes
Cooking time: 60 to 70 minutes
Serves 6

> 1 prepared pie crust, homemade or store-bought
> 2 cups cooked cannelini beans
> ¹/₄ cup, plus 2 tablespoons sugar
> ¹/₄ cup low-fat milk
> 1 egg
> 2 teaspoons grated lemon zest
> 1 teaspoon almond or vanilla extract
> 1 12-ounce package frozen raspberries, defrosted slightly
> 2 tablespoons sugar
> 1 tablespoon cornstarch
> 2 tablespoons sliced almonds

1. Preheat oven to 375°F. Prick bottom and sides of crust and bake until it is just beginning to color, 10 to 12 minutes. Reduce oven temperature to 350°F.

2. Meanwhile, combine beans, ¹/₄ cup of sugar, milk, egg, lemon zest, and almond extract in a food processor and process until smooth. *(Continued on next page)*

3. Toss raspberries with remaining sugar and cornstarch. Spread $1/2$ of raspberry mixture on bottom of crust. Pour bean mixture over them and dot top with remaining raspberry mixture. Sprinkle with almonds.

4. Bake for 50 to 60 minutes until filling is firm and lightly golden on top.

MOLASSES BEAN SOUFFLÉ WITH LEMON-GINGER SAUCE

Don't let this recipe intimidate you. It's easy to make and is a perfect ending to a winter meal.

Preparation time: 10 minutes
Cooking time: 35 to 40 minutes
Serves 5 to 6

Soufflé:

2 cups cooked pinto beans
1 cup low-fat milk
1/2 cup molasses
2 tablespoons sherry
1 tablespoon chopped ginger
1 tablespoon vegetable oil
1 teaspoon allspice
1/2 teaspoon nutmeg
1/4 teaspoon ground cloves
3 egg whites

Sauce:

1/4 cup lemon juice
1/4 cup sugar
3 tablespoons sherry
3 tablespoons currants
1 tablespoon grated ginger

1. Preheat oven to 325°F.

(*Continued on next page*)

2. In a food processor, combine beans, milk, molasses, sherry, oil, ginger, allspice, nutmeg, and cloves. Process until smooth and transfer mixture to a large bowl.

3. Beat egg whites until stiff and gently fold them into bean mixture. Pour batter into a 1-quart baking dish. Bake until puffed and golden, 35 to 40 minutes.

4. To prepare sauce: Combine lemon juice, sugar, sherry, currants, and ginger in a small saucepan. Heat to boiling over medium flame, stirring constantly. Cook until currants are plump, about 3 minutes.

5. Serve soufflé warm, drizzled with sauce.

ORANGY RICE AND BEAN PUDDING

This pudding is gratefully dedicated to Marie Simmons, author of *Rice: The Amazing Grain,* and rice pudding maker extraordinaire! Served warm or cold it makes a delicious dessert or breakfast treat.

Preparation time: 5 minutes
Cooking time: 45 to 50 minutes
Serves 4 to 6

  2 teaspoons vegetable oil
  1 cup long-grain brown rice
  1 tablespoon chopped orange zest
  1-inch cinnamon stick
  2$^1/_2$ cups water
  $^1/_4$ cup, plus 1 tablespoon sugar
  2 cups cooked adzuki beans
  $^3/_4$ cup low-fat milk
  $^1/_2$ cup diced orange segments, pith removed
  $^1/_2$ teaspoon vanilla extract
  Ground cinnamon, to garnish

1. Heat oil in a large saucepan over medium-low flame. Add rice, orange zest, and cinnamon stick. Stir to coat. Stir in water and 1 tablespoon sugar, and bring mixture to a boil. Reduce heat and simmer, covered, for 30 minutes.

2. Add beans to rice, stir once, and continue cooking until rice is tender. If there is still liquid in the pan, in-

crease heat and stir until the excess water has evaporated.

3. Stir milk and remaining sugar into rice and bean mixture. Cook over medium-low heat, stirring frequently, until very thick, 10 to 15 minutes. Add orange segments and cool, as desired. Before serving, stir in vanilla and sprinkle with cinnamon.

SOYBEAN GRANOLA

This crunchy and chewy treat can be eaten with milk or yogurt for breakfast, or as a snack, anytime. Soybeans are packed with protein and are a delicious and healthful replacement for the nuts of the classic granola.

Preparation time: 10 minutes
Cooking time: 30 to 35 minutes
Makes 3 cups

$^1/_2$ **pound cooked soybeans**
1$^1/_2$ cups old-fashioned oats
$^1/_2$ **cup raisins**
$^1/_2$ **teaspoon ground cinnamon**
Pinch nutmeg
$^1/_4$ **cup honey**
2 tablespoons molasses
1 tablespoon vegetable oil

1. Preheat oven to 350°F. Place cooked soybeans in a large bowl and cover with plenty of water. Rub beans gently to remove their hulls. Pour off water and hulls. Rinse as necessary. Drain well and dry.

2. Combine beans with oats, raisins, cinnamon, and nutmeg, and set aside.

3. Heat honey, molasses, and oil over a low flame until liquidy. Pour mixture over soybeans and oats. Toss gently until completely coated. Pour mixture onto a nonstick baking sheet and bake, tossing gently every 10 minutes, until golden brown, 30 to 35 minutes. Cool.

INDEX

ABOUT THE AUTHORS

Tamara Holt

An innovative caterer and professional recipe developer, Tamara Holt has a special flair for making healthful foods elegant and easy. Her training includes apprentice work at the New School Culinary Arts Program and recipe development and testing for several well-known cookbook authors. Tamara Holt is also the author of *Broccoli Power* in this series. She lives and works in New York City.

Marilynn Larkin

Marilynn Larkin is an award-winning medical journalist whose articles have appeared in a wide range of national consumer magazines and medical trade publications. She is a contributing editor for *Nutrition Forum* and a former contributing editor for *Health* magazine. She is also the author of two books to be published in the Dell Medical Library, *What You Can Do About Anemia* and *Relief From Chronic Sinusitis*. Marilynn Larkin lives and works in New York City.